GABRIEL GARCÍA MÁRQUEZ

I'm Not Here to Give a Speech

Gabriel García Márquez was born in Colombia in 1927. He was awarded the Nobel Prize in Literature in 1982. He is the author of many works of fiction and nonfiction, including *One Hundred Years of Solitude*, *Love in the Time of Cholera*, *The Autumn of the Patriarch*, *The General in His Labyrinth*, and *News of a Kidnapping*. He died in 2014.

INTERNATIONAL

I'm Not Here
to Give a Speech

GABRIEL GARCÍA MÁRQUEZ

Translated by
EDITH GROSSMAN

VINTAGE INTERNATIONAL
Vintage Books
A Division of Penguin Random House LLC
New York

FIRST VINTAGE INTERNATIONAL EDITION, JANUARY 2019

Cataloging-in-Publication data is available from the Library of Congress.

Vintage International Trade Paperback ISBN: 978-1-101-91118-1
eBook ISBN: 978-1-101-91121-1

www.vintagebooks.com

Printed in the United States of America
10   9   8   7   6   5   4   3   2   1

PREFACE TO THE ENGLISH EDITION

Gabriel García Márquez (1927–2014) was one of the most influential figures in twentieth-century literature. Winner of a Nobel Prize in 1982, he was a formidable storyteller, essayist, critic, screenwriter, and journalist, and one of the great thinkers of our time. As a novelist, García Márquez shaped the magical realism movement and paved the way for countless contemporaries and successors, creating narrative worlds rich with meaning and symbolism. His body of work includes such novels as *One Hundred Years of Solitude*, *Love in the Time of Cholera*, *Memories of My Melancholy Whores*, and *Of Love and Other Demons*, as well as non-fiction works such as *News of a Kidnapping* and the autobiographical *Living to Tell the Tale*.

During his life, Márquez spoke publicly and passionately on the issues that interested him. *I'm Not Here to Give a Speech* is a collection of these speeches spanning the length of his career. It offers unique insight into the extraordinary mind that created some of the world's most beloved novels and a final chance to hear the distinctive voice of Gabriel García Márquez. Most of these speeches are translated and published here for the first time in English. Notes on the background to each one are given on pp. 143–54.

THE ACADEMY OF DUTY

Zipaquirá, Colombia, November 17, 1944

Generally, at all social events like this one, a person is designated to give a speech. That person always looks for the most appropriate subject and then develops it for those in attendance. I'm not here to give a speech. For today I've chosen the noble subject of friendship. But what could I tell you about friendship? I might have filled a few pages with anecdotes and aphorisms that in the long run would not have led me to the desired goal. Each of you should analyse your own emotions, consider one by one the reasons why you feel an incomparable preference for the person in whom you have confided all your most private thoughts, and then you will know the reason behind this ceremony.

The chain of ordinary events that has joined us with unbreakable bonds to this group of boys who today will begin to make their way in life, that is friendship. And that is what I would have talked to you about today. But, I repeat, I'm not here to give a speech, and I want only to appoint you the honest judges in this proceeding and invite you to share with the student body of this institution a sad moment of farewell.

Here they are, ready to leave: Henry Sánchez, the appealing d'Artagnan of sports, with his three musketeers, Jorge Fajardo, Augusto Londoño, and Hernando Rodríguez. Here are Rafael Cuenca and Nicolás Reyes, one like the shadow of the other. Here are Ricardo González, the great knight of test tubes, and Alfredo García Romero, declared a dangerous individual in the field of every dispute: together, their lives exemplify true friendship. Here are Julio Villafañe and Rodrigo Restrepo, members of our parliament and our journalism. Here are Miguel Ángel Lozano and Guillermo Rubio, apostles of precision. And here, Humberto Jaimes and Manuel Arenas and Samuel Huertas and Ernesto Martínez, consuls of devotion and goodwill. Here is Álvaro Nivia with his good humour and intelligence. Here are Jaime Fonseca and Héctor Cuéllar and Alfredo Aguirre, three different people and only one true ideal: victory. Here, Carlos Aguirre and Carlos Alvarado, united by the same name and the same desire to be the pride of their nation. And here are Álvaro Baquero and Ramiro Cárdenas and Jaime Montoya, inseparable companions of books. And, finally, here are Julio César Morales and Guillermo Sánchez, like two living pillars who bear on their shoulders the responsibility for my words when I say that this group of boys is destined to endure in the best daguerreotypes in Colombia. All of them are going in search of the light, impelled by the same ideal.

Now that you have heard the qualities of each, I'm going to offer the verdict that you as honest judges must consider: in the name of the Liceo Nacional and of society, I declare this group of young men, in the words of Cicero, regular members of the academy of duty and citizens of intelligence.

Honourable public, the proceeding has concluded.

HOW I BEGAN TO WRITE

Caracas, Venezuela, May 3, 1970

First of all, forgive me for speaking to you seated, but the truth is that if I stand, I run the risk of collapsing with fear. Really. I always thought I was fated to spend the most terrible five minutes of my life on a plane, before twenty or thirty people, and not like this, before two hundred friends. Fortunately, what is happening to me right now allows me to begin to speak about my literature, since I was thinking that I began to be a writer in the same way I climbed up on this platform: I was coerced. I confess I did all I could not to attend this assembly: I tried to get sick, I attempted to catch pneumonia, I went to the barber, hoping he'd slit my throat, and, finally, it occurred to me to come here without a jacket and tie so they wouldn't let me into a meeting as serious as this one, but I forgot I was in Venezuela, where you can go anywhere in shirtsleeves. The result: here I am, and I don't know where to start. But I can tell you, for example, how I began to write.

It had never occurred to me that I could be a writer, but in my student days Eduardo Zalamea Borda, editor of the literary supplement of *El Espectador*, in Bogotá, published a note in which he said that the younger generation of writers had nothing to offer, that a new short-story writer, a new novelist, could not be seen anywhere. And he concluded by declaring that he was often reproached because his paper published only the very well-known names of old writers and nothing by the young, whereas the truth, he said, was that no young people were writing.

Then a feeling of solidarity with my generational companions arose in me, and I resolved to write a story simply to shut the mouth of Eduardo Zalamea Borda, who was my great friend or, at least, became my great friend later. I sat down, wrote the story, and sent it to *El Espectador*. I had my second shock the following Sunday when I opened the paper and there was my full-page story with a note in which

Eduardo Zalamea Borda acknowledged that he had been wrong, because obviously with 'that story the genius of Colombian literature had emerged', or something along those lines.

This time I really did get sick, and I said to myself: 'What a mess I've got myself into! What do I do now so Eduardo Zalamea Borda won't look bad?' Keep on writing was the answer. I always had to face the problem of subjects: I was obliged to find the story before I could write it.

And this allows me to tell you something that I can verify now, after having published five books: the job of writer is perhaps the only one that becomes more difficult the more you do it. The ease with which I sat down one afternoon to write that story can't be compared to the work it costs me now to write a page. As for my method of working, it's fairly consistent with what I'm telling you now. I never know how much I'll be able to write or what I'm going to write about. I hope I'll think of something, and when I do come up with an idea that I consider good enough to write down, I begin to go over it in my mind and let it keep maturing. When it's finished (and sometimes many years go by, as in the case of

One Hundred Years of Solitude, which I thought over for nineteen years) – I repeat, when it's finished – then I sit down to write it, and that's when the most difficult part begins, and the part that bores me most. Because the most delicious part of a story is thinking about it, rounding it out, turning it over and over, so that when the time comes to sit down and write it, it doesn't interest you very much, or at least it doesn't interest me very much, the idea that's been turned over and over.

I'm going to tell you, for example, about the idea that has been turning over and over in my mind for several years, and I suspect I have it pretty rounded out by now. I'll tell it to you because there's no doubt that when I write it, I don't know when, you'll find it completely changed and be able to observe how it evolved. Imagine a very small village where there's an old woman who has two children, a boy seventeen and a girl not yet fourteen. She's serving her children breakfast with a very worried look on her face. Her children ask what's wrong and she replies: 'I don't know, but I woke up thinking that something very serious is going to happen in this village.'

They laugh at her and say those are an old woman's misgivings, just something that will pass. The boy goes out to play billiards, and as he's about to shoot a very simple cannon, his opponent says: 'I'll bet you a peso you can't make the shot.' Everybody laughs, he laughs, takes his shot, and doesn't make it. He gives a peso to his opponent, who asks: 'But what happened? It was a really simple cannon.' He says: 'It was, but I'm worried about something my mother said this morning about something serious that's going to happen in this village.' Everybody laughs at him, and the one who won the peso goes home, where he finds his mother and a cousin or a niece, or some female relative. Happy about his peso, he says: 'I won this peso from Dámaso in the simplest way because he's a fool.' 'And why is he a fool?' He says: 'Oh man, he couldn't make a really simple cannon shot because he was worried about his mother waking up today with the idea that something very serious is going to happen in this village.'

Then his mother says: 'Don't make fun of old people's misgivings, because sometimes they come true.' The relative hears this and goes out to buy meat. She says to the butcher: 'Give me a pound of meat,' and just as he's cutting it, she adds: 'Better make it two, because people are saying that something serious is going to happen and it's best to be prepared.' The butcher hands her the meat and, when another woman comes in to buy a pound of meat, he says: 'Take two, because people are coming in and saying that something very serious is going to happen and they're preparing for it, buying things.'

Then the old woman replies: 'I have several children; look, better give me four pounds.' She takes her four pounds and, to make a long story short, I'll say that in half an hour the butcher sells all his meat, slaughters another cow, sells all of that, and the rumour spreads. The moment arrives when everybody in the village is waiting for something to happen. Activities grind to a halt and, suddenly, at two in the afternoon, it's as hot as it always is. Someone says: 'Have you noticed how hot it is?' 'But in this village it's always hot.' So hot that it's a village where all the musicians had instruments repaired with tar and always played in the shade, because if they played in the sun the instruments fell apart. 'Still,' one person says, 'it's never been so hot at this time of day.' 'Yes, but not as hot as it is now.' And, without warning, a little bird flies down into the deserted village, the deserted square, and the news spreads: 'There's a little bird in the square.' Everybody goes to the square and is frightened when they see the little bird.

'But, my friends, there have always been little birds that fly down.' 'Yes, but never at this time of day.' It is a moment of such tension for the inhabitants of the village that they are all desperate to leave but lack the courage to go. 'Well, I'm a real man,' one of them shouts, 'and I'm leaving.' He gets his furniture, his children, his animals, puts them in a cart, and crosses the main street, where the poor villagers are watching him. Until the moment when they say: 'If he has the courage to leave, well, we're leaving too,' and begin literally to dismantle the village. They take away things, animals, everything. And one of the last to abandon the village says: 'Let no misfortune fall on what remains of our house,' and then he burns his house and others burn other houses. They flee in a real and terrible panic, like an exodus in wartime, and among them is the woman who had the misgiving, crying out: 'I said something very serious was going to happen, and you told me I was crazy.'

BECAUSE OF YOU

Caracas, Venezuela, August 2, 1972

Now that we're alone, among friends, I'd like to request the collaboration of all of you in helping me endure the memory of this evening, the first in my life when I've come in person and with full use of my faculties to do two things at the same time that I'd promised myself I would never do: accept a prize and give a speech.

I've always believed, contrary to other very respectable opinions, that we writers are not in the world to be crowned, and many of you know that each public tribute is the start of being embalmed. I've always believed, after all, that we're writers not through our own merits but because of the misfortune that we can't be anything else, and that our solitary work should not earn us more recompense or privileges than those the shoemaker deserves for making his shoes. However, don't think I've come here to beg your pardon for having come here, or that I'm trying to belittle the distinction given me today under the propitious name of a great and unforgettable man of American letters [Rómulo Gallegos]. On the contrary, I've come to rejoice in the public performance, and for having encountered a reason for breaking my principles and muzzling my scruples: I'm here, friends, simply because of my old, stubborn affection for this land where I was once young, undocumented, and happy, as an act of affection and solidarity with my Venezuelan friends, friends who are generous, damn fine, and wise guys to the death. I've come because of them, that is, because of you.

ANOTHER, DIFFERENT HOMELAND

Mexico City, October 22, 1982

I accept the Order of the Aztec Eagle with two emotions that don't usually go together: pride and gratitude. In this way, the deeply affectionate bond that my wife and I established with this country, where we chose to live more than twenty years ago, has been formalized. Here is where my children grew up, here is where I wrote my books, here is where I planted my trees.

In the sixties, when I was no longer happy but was still undocumented, Mexican friends offered me their support and filled me with the temerity to continue writing in circumstances I evoke today like a chapter in *One Hundred Years of Solitude* that I forgot about. In the past decade, when success and too much publicity were trying to disturb my private life, the discretion and legendary tact of the Mexicans allowed me to find the inner calm and inviolable time to tirelessly pursue with no rest my difficult carpenter's trade. It isn't, then, a second homeland but another, different homeland, given to me without conditions, not competing with my own homeland for the love and fidelity I profess for it and the nostalgia with which it unceasingly claims them.

But the honour granted my person moves me not only because this is the country where I live and have lived. I feel, Mr President, that this distinction from your government also honours all the exiles who have found refuge in the sanctuary of Mexico. I know I have no standing at all, and that my case is anything but typical. I also know that the current conditions of my residence in Mexico are not the same for the immense majority of the persecuted who in this past decade have found in Mexico a providential haven. Unfortunately, there still exist on our continent distant tyrannies and nearby massacres that compel an exile much less voluntary and pleasant than mine. I speak in my own name, but I know that many will recognize themselves in my words.

Thank you, sir, for these open doors. May they never close, please, under any circumstances.

THE SOLITUDE OF LATIN AMERICA

Stockholm, Sweden, December 8, 1982

Antonio Pigafetta, a Florentine navigator who accompanied Magellan on his first voyage around the world, wrote about his passage through our southern America in a rigorous chronicle that still seems to be an imagined adventure. He said he had seen pigs whose navels were on their backs, legless birds whose females hatched their eggs on the shoulders of the males, and others, such as tongueless pelicans whose beaks resembled a spoon. He said he had seen a monstrous animal with the head and ears of a mule, the body of a camel, the feet of a deer, and the whinny of a horse. He said they placed the first native they came across in Patagonia before a mirror and the maddened giant lost the use of his reason because he was terrified by his own image.

This brief, fascinating book, in which there are already glimpses of the beginnings of our novels today, is by no means the most astonishing testimony from that time to our reality. The chroniclers of the Indies left us countless others. El Dorado – our illusory country, so intensely longed for – appeared on numerous maps for many long years, changing location and shape according to the cartographers' fantasy. Searching for the Fountain of Youth, the legendary Álvar Núñez Cabeza de Vaca explored the north of Mexico for eight years on an extraordinary expedition whose members ate one another, and only five survived of the six hundred who started out. One of many unsolved mysteries involves the eleven thousand mules, each carrying one hundred pounds of gold, that left Cuzco one day to pay Atahualpa's ransom and never reached their destination. Later, during the colonial period, hens raised on alluvial plains, their gizzards containing small nuggets of gold, were sold in Cartagena de Indias. This gold fever of our founders pursued us until very recently. Just in the last century, the German mission responsible for studying the construction of an interoceanic railroad on the Isthmus of Panama concluded that the project was viable only if the rails were made not of iron, which was a scarce metal in the region, but of gold.

Independence from Spanish rule did not save us from madness. General Antonio López de Santa Anna, three times the dictator of Mexico, had a magnificent funeral for his right leg, lost in what was called the Pastry War. General Gabriel García Moreno governed Ecuador for sixteen years as an absolute monarch, and a vigil was held for his corpse, which wore his dress uniform and a breast-plate of medals and sat on the presidential chair. General Maximiliano Hernández Martínez, the theosophical despot of El Salvador who extermi-nated thirty thousand peasants in a barbaric slaughter, invented a pendulum to determine whether food was poisoned and had the streetlights covered in red paper to combat an epidemic of scar-let fever. The monument to General Francisco Morazán, erected on the main square of Teguci-galpa, is in reality a statue of Marshal Ney purchased at a warehouse of second-hand sculptures.

Eleven years ago, one of the celebrated poets of our time, the Chilean Pablo Neruda, enlightened this setting with his words. Since then, in the good consciences of Europe, and at times in the bad as well, spectral news of Latin America, that immense homeland of deluded men and historic women whose endless intractability is confused with legend, has erupted with more force than ever. We have not had a moment's peace. A Promethean president entrenched in his burning palace died fighting alone against an entire army, and two suspicious and never clarified aerial disasters cut short the lives of another president with a generous heart and a democratic military man who had restored the dignity of his people.

There have been five wars and seventeen coups, and a Luciferian dictator appeared who in the name of God carried out the first ethnocide in Latin America in our time. Meanwhile, 20 million Latin American children died before their second birthday, more than all the children born in Europe since 1970. Those who have disappeared for reasons of tyranny number almost 120,000, which is as if we did not know today the whereabouts of all the residents of the city of Uppsala. Numerous women arrested when they were pregnant gave birth in Argentine prisons, but the whereabouts and identities of their children, given up for clandestine adoption or placed in orphanages by the military authorities, are still unknown. Because they did not want matters to continue in this way, approximately 200,000 women and men have died throughout the continent, and more than 100,000 perished in three small, intransigent countries in Central America: Nicaragua, El Salvador, and Guatemala. If this had occurred in the United States, the proportional figure would be 1,000,600 violent deaths in four years.

One million people, 10 per cent of its population, have fled Chile, a country with traditions of hospitality. Uruguay, a tiny nation of two and a half million residents, considered the most civilized country on the continent, has lost one out of five citizens to exile. Since 1979, the civil war in El Salvador has produced a refugee almost every twenty minutes. The country that could be formed with all the exiles and forced emigrants of Latin America would have a population larger than that of Norway.

I presume to think that it is this singular reality, and not only its literary expression, that has deserved the attention this year of the Swedish Academy of Letters. A reality not made of paper but one that lives with us and determines every instant of our countless daily deaths, and that sustains a constant surge of insatiable creation, filled with misfortune and beauty, of which this errant, nostalgic Colombian is simply another number marked by good fortune. Poets and beggars, warriors and scoundrels, all of us who are creatures of that disordered reality have had to ask very little of our imaginations, because the greatest challenge for us has been the insufficiency of conventional devices to make our lives believable. This, friends, is the core of our solitude.

If these difficulties hamper us, who are of its essence, it is not difficult to understand that the rational prodigies on this side of the world, enraptured by the contemplation of their own culture, have been left without a valid method for interpreting us. It is understandable that they insist on measuring us with the same yardstick they use to measure themselves, not remembering that the ravages of life are not the same for everyone, and that the search for identity is as arduous and bloody for us as it was for them. The interpretation of our reality using foreign systems only contributes to making us more and more unknown, less and less free, more and more solitary. Perhaps venerable Europe would be more understanding if it tried to see us in its own past. If it remembered that London needed three hundred years to construct its first wall and another three hundred to have a bishop; that Rome struggled for twenty centuries in the darkness of uncertainty before an Etruscan king established it in history; and that even in the sixteenth century, the peaceful Swiss of today, who delight us with their mild cheeses and intrepid clocks, bloodied Europe as soldiers of fortune. Even at the height of the Renaissance, twelve thousand German mercenaries in the pay of imperial armies sacked and devastated Rome and put eight thousand of its residents to the knife.

I do not claim to embody the illusions of Tonio Kröger, whose dreams of union between a chaste north and a passionate south Thomas Mann exalted here fifty-three years ago, but I do believe that

Europeans with an enlightening spirit – those who struggle here as well for a larger homeland that is more humane and more just – could be more helpful to us if they thoroughly revised their way of seeing us. Solidarity with our dreams will not make us feel less alone until it is concretized into acts of legitimate support for peoples who take on the dream of having their own life in the ordering of the world.

Latin America does not want to be, nor is there any reason for it to be, a pawn with no will of its own, and there is nothing chimerical about its plans for independence and originality becoming a Western aspiration. And yet the advances in navigation that have reduced so many distances between our Americas and Europe seem to have increased our cultural distance. Why is the originality granted to us without reservation in literature denied us with every kind of suspicion when we make our extremely difficult attempts at social change? Why think that social justice, which advanced Europeans strive to establish in their own countries, cannot also be a Latin American objective using distinct methods under different conditions? No: the inordinate violence and pain of our history are the result of countless secular injustices and animosities, not a conspiracy hatched three thousand leagues from our home. But many European leaders and thinkers have believed this, with the childishness of grandparents who have forgotten the fruitful madness of their youth, as if no other destiny were possible than living at the mercy of the two great masters of the world. This, friends, is the size of our solitude. And yet, in the face of oppression, pillage, and abandonment, our response is life. Neither floods nor plagues nor famines nor cataclysms, not even eternal wars lasting centuries and centuries, have succeeded in reducing the tenacious advantage of life over death.

An advantage that grows and accelerates: each year there are 74 million more births than deaths, a number of new lives that could increase the population of New York by a factor of seven every year. Most are born in the countries with fewest resources and, among them, of course, are those of Latin America. On the other hand, the most prosperous countries have succeeded in accumulating sufficient destructive power to annihilate a hundred times over not only all the human beings who have existed until now, but the totality of living creatures that have spent time on this planet of misfortunes.

On a day like today, my teacher William Faulkner said in this place: 'I decline to accept the end of man.' I wouldn't feel worthy of occupying this spot that was his if I weren't fully aware that, for the first time since the origin of humankind, the colossal catastrophe that he declined to accept thirty-two years ago is now nothing more than a simple scientific possibility. Faced with this terrifying reality that throughout all of human time must have seemed a fantasy, the inventors of fables we all believe feel we have the right to believe that it still isn't too late to undertake the creation of a contrary utopia. A new, overwhelming utopia of life, where no one can decide for others even how they'll die, where love is really true and happiness possible, and where the peoples condemned to one hundred years of solitude at last and forever have a second chance on earth.

A TOAST TO POETRY

Stockholm, Sweden, December 10, 1982

I thank the Swedish Academy of Letters for favouring me with a prize that places me next to many of those who conditioned and enriched my years as a reader and daily participant in the irremediable delirium of the writing trade. Their names and works appear to me today as tutelary shades, but also as the commitment, often overwhelming, that is acquired with this honour. A difficult honour that seemed like simple justice in them but in me I understand as another of those lessons with which destiny tends to surprise us and which makes even more obvious our condition as the playthings of an indecipherable chance whose only devastating recompense is, most of the time, incomprehension and oblivion.

It is, therefore, only natural, against the secret backdrop where we usually rummage through the most essential truths that shape our identity, that I should ask myself what has been the constant foundation of my work, what could have attracted the attention of this tribunal of extremely severe judges in so compromising a way. I confess with no false modesty that it has not been easy for me to find the reason, but I want to believe it is for the reason I would have desired. I want to believe, my friends, that this is, once again, a tribute paid to poetry. Poetry by whose virtue the prodigious inventory of ships enumerated by old Homer in his *Iliad* are visited by a wind that pushes them to sail with unearthly, dazzling speed. Poetry that sustains, in the slender scaffolding of Dante's tercets, the entire dense, colossal structure of the Middle Ages. Poetry that with such miraculous totality rescues our America in 'The Heights of Macchu Picchu' by Pablo Neruda, the great, the greatest, and where our best dead-end dreams distil their millenarian sorrow. Poetry, in short, the secret energy of daily life that cooks garbanzos in the kitchen and spreads love like a contagion and repeats images in mirrors.

In every line I write I always try, with greater or lesser success, to invoke the elusive spirits of poetry and leave in each word a testimony to my devotion because of its powers of divination and its permanent victory over the muffled powers of death. The prize I have just received I understand, in all humility, as the consoling revelation that my effort has not been in vain. For that reason I invite all of you to toast what a great poet of our Americas, Luis Cardoza y Aragón, has defined as the only concrete proof of the existence of man: poetry. Thank you very much.

WORDS FOR A NEW
MILLENNIUM

Havana, Cuba, November 29, 1985

I've always wondered what meetings of intellectuals were good for. Aside from the very few that
have had real historical significance in our time, like
the one held in Valencia, Spain, in 1937, most of
them are no more than simple salon entertainments.
Still, it's surprising that so many take place, more
and more of them, more crowded and expensive
the more the world crisis deepens. A Nobel Prize in
Literature assures one of receiving in the following
year almost two thousand invitations to writers'
conferences, art festivals, colloquia, seminars of all
kinds: more than three a day in sites scattered
around the world. There's an institutional conference going on constantly, all expenses paid, whose

meetings are held each year in thirty-one different places, some as attractive as Rome or Adelaide, or as surprising as Stavanger or Yverdon, or in some that seem like crossword challenges, like Polyphénix or Knokke. There are so many, in short, about so many different and varied subjects, that during the past year, in Muiden Castle, in Amsterdam, an international conference of organizers of poetry conferences was held. It's not unimaginable: a complaisant intellectual could be born at one conference and continue growing and maturing at successive conferences, with no more respites than those needed to move from one to the other, until he died at a ripe old age at his last conference.

And yet it may be too late to try to break this habit that we artisans of culture have been dragging through history ever since Pindar celebrated the Olympic Games. Those were times when body and spirit were on better terms with each other than they are today, and so the voices of bards were appreciated in stadiums as much as the feats of athletes. The Romans, ever since 508 BCE, must have suspected that abuse of the games was their greatest danger. For at about that time they inaugurated the

Secular Games, and then the Terentini Games, celebrated at intervals that are exemplary for today: every one hundred or one hundred and ten years.

Cultural conferences in the Middle Ages were also debates and tourneys of minstrels, then troubadours, and then minstrels and troubadours at the same time, beginning a tradition that we still often suffer from: they started as games and ended as disputes. But they also reached such splendour that, during the reign of Louis XIV, they opened with a colossal banquet whose evocation here – I swear – is no attempt at a veiled hint: nineteen bullocks were served, three thousand pies, and more than two hundred casks of wine.

The culmination of this performance by minstrels and troubadours was the Floral Games of Toulouse, the oldest and most persistent of poetic competitions, inaugurated 660 years ago – a model of continuity. Its founder, Clemencia Isaura, was an intelligent, enterprising, and beautiful woman, whose only fault seems to have been that she never existed: perhaps she was purely an invention of seven troubadours who created the competition in an effort to prevent the extinction of Provençal poetry. But her very lack of existence is one more proof of the creative power of poetry, for in Toulouse there is a tomb of Clemencia Isaura in the Church of La Dorada, and a street that bears her name, and a monument to her memory.

This being said, we have the right to ask ourselves: what are we doing here? And, above all: what am I doing up on this perch of honour, I who have always considered speeches the most terrifying of human predicaments? I don't have the courage to suggest an answer, but I can offer a proposal: we are here to try to hold a meeting of intellectuals that has what the immense majority of them haven't had – practical utility and continuity.

First, there is something that distinguishes it. In addition to writers, painters, musicians, sociologists, and historians, at this meeting there is a group of distinguished scientists. That is, we have dared to defy the feared collusion of sciences and arts; to mix in the same crucible those of us who still trust in the clairvoyance of omens and those who believe only in verifiable truths: the very ancient antagonism between inspiration and experience, between instinct and reason. Saint-John Perse, in his memorable Nobel Prize acceptance speech, defeated this false dilemma with a single sentence: 'In the scientist as well as in the poet,' he said, 'disinterested thought must be honoured.' Here, at least, let them not be considered as inimical brothers, for the questioning of both is the same over the same abyss.

The idea that science concerns only scientists is as anti-scientific as it is anti-poetic to pretend that poetry concerns only poets. In that sense, the name of UNESCO – United Nations Educational, Scientific and Cultural Organization – limps through the world with a serious inaccuracy, taking as fact that the three are different when, in reality, all of them are a single thing. For culture is the totalizing power of creation: the social development of human intelligence. Or, as Jack Lang said without much ado: 'Culture is everything.' Welcome, then, welcome everyone to everyone's house.

I don't dare to suggest anything more than a few reasons for reflection during these three days of spiritual retreats. I do dare to remind you, first of all, of something you perhaps remember all too well: any decision in the medium term made in these twilight times is a decision for the twenty-first century. And yet, we Latin Americans and people from the Caribbean approach it with the devastating sense that we've skipped the twentieth century: we've passed through it without having lived it. Half the world will celebrate the dawn of the year 2001 as the culmination of a millennium, while we are barely beginning to catch glimpses of the benefits of the Industrial Revolution. The children in primary school today, preparing to govern our destinies in the coming century, are still condemned to counting on their fingers, like the accountants of remotest antiquity, while computers exist that are capable of performing a hundred thousand arithmetical operations a second. On the other hand, in one hundred years we have lost the best human virtues of the nineteenth century: fervent idealism and the primacy of feeling: the shock of love.

At some point in the next millennium genetics will glimpse the eternity of human life as a real possibility, electronic intelligence will dream of the chimerical adventure of writing a new *Iliad*, and in their house on the moon there will be a pair of lovers from Ohio or Ukraine, overwhelmed by nostalgia, who will love each other in glass gardens in the earthlight. Latin America and the Caribbean, on the other hand, seem condemned to servitude to the present: telluric dread, political and social cataclysms, the immediate urgencies of daily life, dependencies of every kind, poverty and injustice, have not left us much time to assimilate the lessons of the past or to think about the future. The Argentine writer Rodolfo Terragno has synthesized this drama: 'We use X-rays and transistors, cathode tubes and electronic memory, but we haven't incorporated the foundations of contemporary culture into our own culture.'

Fortunately, the determinant reserve of Latin America and the Caribbean is an energy capable of moving the world: the dangerous memory of our peoples. It is an immense cultural patrimony that antedates any raw material, a primary material of multiple character that accompanies every step of our lives. It is a culture of resistance expressed in the hiding places of language, in mulatta Virgins – our artisanal patron saints – true miracles of the people against the colonizing clerical power. It is a culture of solidarity expressed in the face of criminal excesses of untamed nature, or in the insurgency of peoples for the sake of their identity and sovereignty. It is a culture of protest in the indigenous faces on artisanal angels in our temples, or in the music of the perpetual snows that attempts to exorcize with nostalgia the silent powers of death. It is a culture of ordinary life expressed in the imagination of cooking, in styles of dress, in creative superstition, in the intimate liturgies of love. It is a culture of fiesta, of transgression, of mystery, which breaks the straitjacket of reality and at last reconciles reason and imagination, word and act, and actually demonstrates that there is no concept that sooner or later is not exceeded by life. This is the strength of our backwardness. An energy of novelty and beauty that belongs to us in its entirety and with which we ourselves are sufficient; it cannot be domesticated by imperial voracity, or by the brutality of the internal oppressor, or even by our own immemorial fears of translating into words our most cherished dreams. Even the revolution itself is a cultural work, the total expression of a creative vocation and a creative capability that justify and demand of all of us a profound confidence in the future.

This would be something more than just another of the many meetings that occur every day in the world if we were able to catch even a glimpse of new forms of practical organization to channel the irresistible flood of creativity of our peoples, real exchange and solidarity among our creators, historical continuity, and a broader, deeper social usefulness for intellectual creation, the most mysterious and solitary of all human occupations. It would be, in brief, a decisive contribution to the political determination, which cannot be deferred, to leap over five alien centuries and enter, with a firm step and a thousand-year horizon, the imminent millennium.

THE CATACLYSM OF DAMOCLES

Ixtapa–Zihuatanejo, Mexico, August 6, 1986

One minute after the final explosion, more than half the human race will have died, the dust and smoke from the continents in flames will vanquish the sunlight, and absolute darkness will once again rule the world. A winter of orange rains and icy hurricanes will reverse the weather of the oceans and change the course of the rivers, whose fish will have died of thirst in the burning waters and whose birds will not find the sky. Perpetual snows will cover the Sahara Desert, vast Amazonia will disappear from the face of the planet, destroyed by hail, and the age of rock music and transplanted hearts will return to its glacial infancy. The few humans who may survive their terror, and those who had the privilege of safe refuge at three in the afternoon on the fateful Monday of the extreme catastrophe, will have saved their lives only to die afterwards because of the horror of their memories. Creation will have ended. In the final chaos of rains and eternal night, the only vestige of what life once was will be the cockroach.

Honourable presidents, honourable prime ministers, friends:

This is not a poor imitation of John's delirium in his exile on Patmos, but the expected vision of a cosmic disaster that can occur at this very moment: the explosion – intentional or accidental – of only a tiny part of the nuclear arsenal that sleeps with one eye open in the weapons depositories of the great powers.

This is true. Today, August 6, 1986, there are more than fifty thousand nuclear warheads in place in the world. In simple terms, this means that each human being, including children, sits on a barrel holding four tons of dynamite whose total explosion can eliminate every trace of life on Earth twelve times over. The power to annihilate of this colossal threat that hangs over our heads like a cataclysm of Damocles raises the theoretical possibility of devastating four other planets that circle the sun, affecting the equilibrium of the solar system. No science, no art, no industry has doubled its size as many times as the nuclear industry since its beginnings forty-one years ago, nor has any other creation of human ingenuity ever had as much power to determine the fate of the world.

The only consolation in these terrifying simplifications – if they are of any use to us at all – is confirming that the preservation of human life on Earth continues to be cheaper than the nuclear plague, for merely by existing the awful Apocalypse held captive in the silos of death in the richest countries is squandering the possibilities of a better life for everyone.

In child welfare, for example, this is an elementary mathematical truth. In 1981, UNICEF calculated the cost of a programme to resolve the essential problems of the 500 million poorest children in the world. It included basic health care, elementary education, improvement of sanitary conditions, and a supply of potable water and food.

All this seemed an impossible dream of $100 billion. However, that is barely the cost of a hundred B-1B strategic bombers, and less than the price of seven thousand cruise missiles, in whose production the government of the United States will invest $21,200 million.

In health, for example: with the price of ten Nimitz atomic aircraft carriers of the fifteen the United States is going to manufacture before the year 2000, a preventive programme could be carried out that would protect, in those same fourteen years, more than 1 billion people against malaria and prevent the death – in Africa alone – of more than 14 million children.

In nutrition, for example: last year there were in the world, according to the calculations of the Food and Agriculture Organization of the United Nations, some 575 million hungry people. Their average indispensable caloric intake would cost less than 149 MX missiles of the 223 that will be in place in Western Europe. Twenty-seven of them would buy the agricultural machinery needed so that poor countries could acquire food self-sufficiency in the next four years. Further, that programme would not cost even a ninth of the Soviet military budget for 1982.

In education, for example: with only two Trident nuclear submarines of the twenty-five the current government of the United States plans to manufacture, or with a similar quantity of the Typhoon submarines the Soviet Union is building, the fantasy of worldwide literacy could finally be attempted. And the construction of schools and the teacher training the Third World will need to meet additional educational demands in the next ten years could be paid for at the cost of 245 Trident II missiles, and there would still be 419 missiles left over for the same increase in education in the following fifteen years.

Finally, it can be said that the cancellation of the foreign debt of the entire Third World, and its economic recovery for ten years, would cost little more than a sixth of the world's military expenditures over the same period of time. All in all, faced with this enormous economic waste, the human waste is even sadder and more disturbing: the industry of war keeps in captivity the greatest impounding of learned people ever gathered together for any enterprise in human history. Our people, whose natural place isn't there but here, at this table, and whose liberation is indispensable so they can help us to create, in the area of education and justice, the only thing that can save us from barbarism: a culture of peace.

In spite of these dramatic certainties, the arms race does not concede a moment's pause. Now, while we were having lunch, a new nuclear warhead was built. Tomorrow, when we awake, there will be nine more in the warehouses of death in the hemisphere of the wealthy. All in all, what just one of them costs would be enough – even if it were for only one Sunday in autumn – to perfume Niagara Falls with sandalwood.

A great novelist of our time once wondered whether Earth wasn't the hell of other planets. Perhaps it is much less: a hamlet without memory, left by the hands of its gods in the farthest suburb of the great universal homeland. But the growing suspicion is that it is the only place in the solar system where the prodigious adventure of life drags us without mercy to a disheartening conclusion: the arms race is contrary to intelligence.

And not only human intelligence, but the intelligence of nature itself, whose purpose escapes even the clairvoyance of poetry. Since the appearance of visible life on Earth, 380 million years had to go by to make a rose with no other commitment than to be beautiful, and four geological eras for human beings – unlike their pithecanthropic great-grandfather – to be able to sing better than the birds and to die of love. It does no honour to human talent, in the golden age of science, to have conceived of the way in which so extravagant and huge a multi-millennial process can return to the nothingness it came from by the simple art of pressing a button.

We are here to try to stop that from happening, joining our voices to the countless others that call for a world without armaments and a peace with justice. But even if it happens – even more so if it happens – our being here will not have been in vain. Millions and millions of millennia after the explosion, a triumphant salamander that will have again travelled the complete ladder of species will perhaps be crowned as the most beautiful woman of the new creation. It depends on us, men and women of science, men and women of arts and letters, men and women of intelligence and peace, it depends on all of us that the guests at that chimerical coronation do not attend their celebration with the same terror we feel today. With all modesty, but also with all the determination of my spirit, I propose that here and now we commit ourselves to conceiving and building an ark of memory capable of surviving the atomic flood. A bottle of shipwrecked sailors in space thrown into the oceans of time so that the new humanity will know through us what the cockroaches won't tell them: that here life existed, that in it suffering prevailed and injustice predominated, but that we also knew love and were even capable of imagining happiness. And let them know, and let it be known for all time, the ones who were responsible for our disaster, and how deaf they became to our cries for peace so that this could be the best of all possible lives, and with what barbarous inventions and for the sake of what paltry interests they erased it from the universe.

AN INDESTRUCTIBLE IDEA

Havana, Cuba, December 4, 1986

It all began with those two pylons at the entrance to this house. Two horrible pylons, like two giraffes of barbaric concrete, which a heartless bureaucrat ordered planted in the front garden without even warning the legitimate owners, and which sustain over our heads, at this very moment, a high-tension current of 110 million volts, enough to keep a million television sets turned on or to support 23,000 35-millimetre movie projectors. Alarmed at the news, President Fidel Castro came here six months ago, trying to see if there was some way to correct the injustice, and this was how we discovered that the house could shelter the dreams of the Foundation of the New Latin American Cinema.

The pylons are still there, of course, more and more hateful as the house has been made more beautiful. We have tried to mask them with royal palms, with flowering branches, but their ugliness is so obvious that it prevails over every artifice. The only thing we can think of, as a final recourse to turn our defeat into victory, is to beg you to see them not as what they are but as a hopeless sculpture.

Only after adopting it as the seat of the Foundation of the New Latin American Cinema did we learn that the story of this house did not begin or end with these pylons, and that a good deal of what is said about it is neither truth nor falsehood. It is cinema. Well, as you must have already surmised, it was here that Tomás Gutiérrez Alea filmed *The Survivors*, a film that, eight years after its completion and twenty-seven after the triumph of the Cuban Revolution, is not one truth more in the history of the imagination nor one falsehood less in the history of Cuba, but part of this third reality between real life and pure invention which is the reality of cinema.

And few houses could be as auspicious as this one

for undertaking in it our final objective, which is nothing less than achieving the integration of Latin American cinema. That simple and that excessive. And no one could condemn us for the simplicity but only for the excess of our initial steps in this first year of life, which happens to be celebrated today, the day of Santa Bárbara, which, through the arts of sainthood or *santería*, is the original name of this house.

Next week the Foundation of the New Latin American Cinema will receive from the Cuban state a grant for which we are eternally grateful, as much for its unprecedented generosity and timeliness as for the personal dedication devoted to it by the least-well-known film enthusiast in the world: Fidel Castro. I am referring to the International School of Film and Television, in San Antonio de los Baños, established to train professionals from Latin America, Asia, and Africa, using the best resources of current technology. The construction of the centre is complete only eight months after it was begun. Instructors from countries throughout the world have been appointed, students have been selected, and most of them are here with us now.

Fernando Birri, the director of the school, who is not distinguished by his sense of unreality, described it not long ago in the presence of the Argentine president, Raúl Alfonsín – and not a muscle in his saint's face twitched – as 'the best school of film and television in the history of the world'.

By its very nature, this will be the most important and ambitious of our initiatives, but it won't be the only one, for the training of professionals without a job would be too expensive a method for encouraging unemployment. And so in this first year we have started to lay the foundation of a vast undertaking to promote the enrichment of the creative environment in Latin American film and television. The initial steps are these:

We have coordinated with private producers in the production of two full-length features and three long documentaries, all of them under the leadership of Latin American filmmakers, and a package of five one-hour stories for television, realized by five film or television directors from various Latin American countries.

At present we are holding meetings to assist young Latin American filmmakers who have not been able to carry out or complete their film or television projects.

We have moved forward with negotiations to acquire a screening room in every country in Latin America, and perhaps in some European capitals as well, devoted to the permanent viewing and study of Latin American film from all periods.

In each country in Latin America we are promoting an annual meeting of film lovers, through the respective sections of the foundation, as a way to obtain advance notification of those who have a vocation, and as a means for the International School of Film and Television to select future students.

We are sponsoring scholarly research into the status of film and television in Latin America, the creation of an audio-visual databank of Latin American cinema, and the first film library of Third World independent cinema.

We are sponsoring the development of a definitive history of Latin American film, and a dictionary to unify cinematographic and television vocabulary in the Spanish language.

The Mexican section of the foundation has

already initiated the publication that compiles, country by country, the principal articles and documents of the New Latin American Cinema.

Within the framework of this Film Festival in Havana, we propose to call on the governments of Latin America and their cinematic entities to begin to think creatively about certain points in their laws that protect national film industries, which in many cases hinder more than they protect and in general terms are contrary to the integration of Latin American cinema.

Between 1952 and 1955 four of us who are aboard this ship today were studying at the Centre of Experimental Cinematography in Rome: Julio García Espinosa, deputy minister of culture for film; Fernando Birri, supreme pontiff of the New Latin American Cinema; Tomás Gutiérrez Alea, one of its most notable goldsmiths; and I, who in those days wanted nothing more in this life than to be the film director I never became. Even back then we talked, almost as much as we do today, about the films that had to be made in Latin America and about how that would be done, and our thoughts were inspired by Italian neo-realism, which is – as ours would have to be — the most human cinema with the fewest resources that has ever been made. But, above all, even then we were aware that Latin American cinema, if it really wanted to exist, could only be one cinema. I'd like to point out that our still being here this evening, talking about the same thing, like madmen who haven't changed the subject in thirty years, and that so many Latin Americans from different places and generations are with us, talking about the same thing, is one more proof of the inescapable power of an indestructible idea.

In those days in Rome I had my only adventure on a cinematic directing team. In school I was chosen as third assistant to the director Alessandro Blasetti for the film *Too Bad She's Bad*, and this brought me great joy, not so much for my personal progress as for the opportunity to meet the lead actress, Sophia Loren. But I never saw her, because for a month my work consisted of holding up a rope at the street corner so that onlookers couldn't walk by. It is with this certificate of good service, and not with the many pretentious ones I have for my work as a novelist, that I now dare to be so much more of a president in this house than I ever have been in my own, and to speak in the name of so many meritorious film people.

This is your house, everyone's house, and the only thing missing to make it complete is a sign visible throughout the world, one that says in compelling letters: 'DONATIONS ACCEPTED'. Come in.

PREFACE TO A NEW MILLENNIUM

Caracas, Venezuela, March 4, 1990

This bold exhibition opens at a historic moment, when humanity is beginning to be different. When Milagros Maldonado conceived of it some three years ago, the world was still in the shadow of the twentieth century, one of the grimmest in this moribund millennium. Thought was captive to irreconcilable dogmas and utilitarian ideologies sown on paper and not in people's hearts, and whose greatest manifestation was the conformist fiction that we were in the plenitude of the human adventure. Then a sudden strong wind from no one knows where began to break apart that colossus with feet of clay, making us understand that we had been on the wrong road for who knows how long.

But, contrary to how it might appear, this is not the prelude to turmoil but just the opposite: the long dawning of a world presided over by the total liberation of thought, so that no one is ruled by anyone other than his or her own mind.

Perhaps our pre-Columbian ancestors had an experience similar to this one in 1492, when a party of European navigators found themselves in these lands that blocked the way to the Indies. Our remote grandparents did not know about gunpowder or the compass, but they could talk to birds and see the future in earthenware bowls, and perhaps they suspected, looking at the stars in the immense nights of their time, that the Earth was as round as an orange, for they were ignorant of the great secrets of today's knowledge but were already masters of the imagination.

This was how they defended themselves against the invaders, with the living legend of El Dorado, a fantastic empire whose king submerged himself in the sacred pool, his body covered in gold dust. The invaders asked them where it was, and the ancestors pointed out the way with five fingers extended. 'This way, that way, over yonder,' they replied.

The paths multiplied, became confused, changed direction, always more distant, always over yonder, always just a little farther. They became as impossible as it was possible for the searchers, maddened by greed, to keep going and lose their way with no roads back. No one ever found El Dorado, no one saw it, it never existed, but its birth put an end to the Middle Ages and opened the way for one of the great eras in the world. Just its name indicated the extent of the change: the Renaissance.

Five centuries later, humanity must have felt once more the shudder of another new age beginning when Neil Armstrong left his footprint on the moon. In a summer house on Pantelleria, a deserted island south of Sicily, our hearts were in our mouths as we watched on television as that almost mythical boot searched blindly for the lunar surface. We were two European couples, with their children, and two couples from Latin America with ours. At the end of an intense wait, the extralunar boot placed its sole on the icy dust and the announcer recited the phrase that must have been thought about since the beginning of time: 'For the first time in the history of humankind, a human being has set foot on the moon.' We were all levitating at the awesomeness of history. All except the Latin American children, who asked in a chorus: 'But is it the first time?' And they left the room feeling cheated: 'How stupid!' For them, everything that had ever passed through their imaginations – like El Dorado – had the value of an accomplished fact. The conquest of space, just as they had supposed it in the cradle, had already happened a long time ago. And happened only once.

And so, in the world of the near future, nothing will be written ahead of time and there will be no place for any consecrated illusion. Many things that were true yesterday will not be true tomorrow. Perhaps formal logic will be degraded to a method used in schools so that children will understand what the ancient, abolished custom of being wrong was like, and maybe the immense, complex technology of current communications will be simplified by telepathy. It will be a kind of enlightened primitivism whose essential tool will be the imagination.

We are entering, then, the era of Latin America, the world's leading producer of creative imagination, the richest, most necessary raw material in the new world, of which these one hundred paintings by one hundred visionary painters can be much more than a sample: they can be the great harbinger of a still-undiscovered continent, where death will be defeated by happiness and there will be more peace for ever, more time, better health, more hot food, more tasty rumbas, more of everything good for everybody. In two words: more love.

I'M NOT HERE

Havana, Cuba, December 8, 1992

This morning, in a European newspaper, I read the news that I'm not here. It didn't surprise me, because earlier I'd heard that I had already removed the furniture, books, records, and paintings from the palace Fidel Castro had given me, and that, through an embassy, I was taking out the original of a novel harshly critical of the Cuban Revolution.

If you didn't know, you do now. Perhaps this is the reason I can't be here this afternoon to open this screening room which, like films, and like everyone who has anything to do with films, may be nothing more than an optical illusion. For this room has cost us so many shocks and uncertainties that today – five hundred years, one month, and twenty-six days after

59

the arrival of Columbus – we can't believe it's really true.

At different times in this story several miracles occurred, but one was definitive: the remarkable scientific development of the country. It was another of the great illusions that became reality around this house. No movie theatre has ever had such brilliant and generous neighbours. When this screening room really seemed doomed not to exist, they knocked at our door, not to ask us for something but to offer us a hand. It is for that reason that the Foundation of the New Latin American Cinema, in just reciprocity, today shares the use of this auditorium with the scientific community in Cuba, certain that we have a great deal to say to one another. This isn't new: Saint-John Perse, in his splendid Nobel Prize acceptance speech, demonstrated how much the sources and methods of the sciences and the arts have in common. As you see, considering that I'm not here, I've been able to tell you quite a lot. I hope this inspires me to bring back my furniture, my books, and my stories, and that Torricelli's equation would please allow us to bring from somewhere else other foundation stones for many more projects like this one.

IN HONOUR OF BELISARIO BETANCUR ON THE OCCASION OF HIS SEVENTIETH BIRTHDAY

Santafé de Bogotá, Colombia, February 18, 1993

Because of a mistake in calculating the time zone, I called the Presidential Palace at three in the morning. The intrusiveness seemed even more alarming when I heard the president in person on the phone. 'Don't worry about it,' he said in his bishop's cadence. 'This job is so complicated that now is the only time I have to read poetry.' For that's what President Belisario Betancur was up to during those tremulous small hours of power: rereading the mathematical verses of Don Pedro Salinas, before the newspapers arrived to embitter the new day with the fantasies of real life.

Nine hundred years ago, William IX, Duke of Aquitaine, also stayed awake on the nights before battle composing libertine *sirventes* and love ballads. Henry VIII – who devastated incomparable libraries and beheaded Thomas More – ended up in anthologies of the Elizabethan period. Tsar Nicholas I helped Pushkin correct his poems to prevent him from stumbling upon the ruthless censorship the Tsar himself had imposed. History did not prove as truculent with Belisario Betancur because in reality he wasn't a ruler who loved poetry but a poet on whom destiny had imposed the penance of power. A ruling vocation whose first pitfall he encountered when he was twelve, in the seminary of Yarumal. This is what happened: fatigued by the dryness of *rosa rosae rosarum*, Belisario wrote his first verses clearly inspired by Quevedo before he'd read Quevedo, and in masterly octosyllables before he'd read González.

> O Lord, O Lord, to Thee we pray
> And we shall pray forevermore,
> To please send down your rays of shit
> Upon our Latin professor.

The first one fell on him, with his immediate expulsion. And God knew very well what He was doing. If this hadn't happened, who knows whether today we would be celebrating the seventieth birthday of the first Colombian pope.

Young people today cannot imagine to what extent we lived back then in the shadow of poetry. We didn't say first year of the baccalaureate but first year of literature, and the degree granted in spite of chemistry and trigonometry was bachelor of letters. For us, aborigines from all the provinces, Bogotá was not the capital of the country or the seat of government but the city of freezing drizzle where the poets lived. We not only believed in poetry but we knew with certainty – as Luis Cardoza y Aragón would say – that it is the only concrete proof of the existence of man. Colombia entered the twentieth century almost half a century late because of poetry. It was a frenzied passion, another way of experiencing a kind of fireball that moved everywhere on its own: you lifted the rug with the broom to hide the dirt and you couldn't because poetry was already there; you opened the paper, even the business section or the police reports, and there it was; in the sediment in our coffee cup, where our fate was written, there it was. Even in the soup. Eduardo Carranza found it there: 'The eyes that look at one another through the domestic angels of steam from the soup'. Jorge Rojas found it in the ludic pleasure of a magisterial quip: 'Mermaids don't spread their legs because the scales made them think there was something fishy.' Daniel Arango found it in a perfect hendecasyllable written in compelling letters on the show window of a store: 'the total fulfilment of your existence'. It was even in the public urinals where the Romans hid it: 'If you don't fear God, fear syphilis.' With the same reverential terror we felt as children when we went to the zoo, we would go to the café where the poets met at dusk. Maestro León de Greiff taught us to lose at chess without rancour, never to give in to a hangover, and, above all, not to be afraid of words. That's the city Belisario Betancur came to when he began the adventure of the world, in a crowd of untamed Antiochians, wearing his felt hat with a brim as wide as a bat's wings and the priest's overcoat that distinguished him from all other mortals. He came to stay in the poets' café and was right at home.

From then on, history would not give him a minute's peace. And as we know very well, even less so in the presidency of the republic, which was perhaps his only act of infidelity to poetry. No other Colombian president had to face at the same time a devastating earthquake, the eruption of a genocidal volcano, and two bloody wars in a Promethean country that for more than a century has been killing itself in its longing to live. I believe, however, that if he managed to sort everything out, it was not only because of his politician's guts, which he has, and very firmly placed, but because of the supernatural power of poets to take on adversity.

It has taken seventy years and the faithlessness of a youthful journal for Belisario finally to reveal himself in the nude, without the many fig leaves of so many colours and sizes that he has used in his life to avoid the risks of being a poet. It is, in the backwater of old age, a worthy and beautiful way to be young again. That is why it seemed so fitting for this gathering of friends to take place in a house of poetry. And, above all, in this one, during whose small hours the secretive steps of José Asunción, kept awake by the sound of the roses, can still be heard, and where many of us, the friends who loved Belisario best from the time before he was president, have met again, we who so often pitied him while he was in office and who continue to love him more than ever now that he has achieved the rare paradise of not holding that office and not wanting to.

MY FRIEND MUTIS

Santafé de Bogotá, Colombia, August 25, 1993

Álvaro Mutis and I had made a pact not to say anything in public, good or bad, about the other, like a
vaccine against the smallpox of mutual praise. And
yet just ten years ago, in this very place, he violated
that public health pact only because he didn't like
the barber I had recommended to him. Since then
I've waited for an opportunity to eat my cold dish
of revenge, and I don't believe there will be another
as auspicious as this one.

At that time Álvaro told how Gonzalo Mallarino
had introduced us in the idyllic Cartagena of 1949.
That encounter really seemed to be our first, until
one afternoon three or four years ago, when I
heard him casually mention something about Felix

Mendelssohn. It was a revelation that all at once transported me to my years as a university student in the deserted music room of the National Library of Bogotá, where those of us who didn't have the five centavos to study in the café took refuge. Among the few patrons at dusk, I hated one with a heraldic nose and the eyebrows of a Turk, an enormous body and shoes as tiny as those of Buffalo Bill, who came in without fail at four in the afternoon and asked for Mendelssohn's Violin Concerto. Forty years had to go by until that afternoon in his house in Mexico City, when without warning I recognized the stentorian voice, the feet of baby Jesus, the trembling hands incapable of passing a needle through the eye of a camel. 'Damn it,' I said to him in defeat. 'So it was you.'

The only thing I regretted was not being able to collect on my overdue resentments because we had already digested so much music together that we had no roads back. And so we continued to be friends, in spite of the unfathomable abyss that yawns in the middle of his vast knowledge and that will separate us for ever: his insensitivity to the bolero.

Álvaro had already endured the many hazards of his countless strange occupations. At the age of eighteen, as an announcer on Radio Nacional, an armed and jealous husband waited for him at the corner because he believed he had detected coded messages to his wife in the presentations Álvaro improvised on his programmes. On another occasion, during a solemn ceremony in this very Presidential Palace, he confused and reversed the names of the two older Lleras. Later, when he was already a specialist in public relations, he showed the wrong film at a benefit and, instead of a documentary about orphaned children he showed the good society ladies a pornographic comedy about nuns and soldiers, disguised by an innocent title: 'Cultivating the Orange'. He was also the head of public relations for an airline that went out of business when its last plane crashed. Álvaro's time was spent identifying bodies in order to notify the victims' families before the newspapers did. The unprepared relatives opened the door, thinking that happiness was calling, and as soon as they saw his face they collapsed with a cry of pain, as if struck by lightning.

In another, more pleasant job he had to remove the elegant corpse of the richest man in the world from a hotel in Barranquilla. He took the body, standing vertically in an emergency coffin purchased at the funeral parlour on the corner, down in the service lift. When the attendant asked him who was inside, he said, 'The most reverend bishop.' In a restaurant in Mexico City, where he was talking in a very loud voice, a man at a nearby table tried to attack him, thinking he really was Walter Winchell, the narrator of *The Untouchables*, whose voice Álvaro had dubbed for television. During his twenty-three years selling canned films for Latin America, he went around the world seventeen times without changing the way he was.

What I've always valued most is his schoolteacher's generosity, for he had a fierce vocation he could never put into practice because of his accursed habit of playing billiards. No writer I know is as concerned as he is for other writers, especially the youngest ones. He incites them to poetry against the will of their parents, perverts them with secret books, hypnotizes them with his florid gift of the gab, and sends them out to wander the world convinced it is possible to be a poet without dying in the attempt.

No one has benefited more than I from that rare virtue. I've already recounted elsewhere that it was Álvaro who gave me my first copy of *Pedro Páramo*, and said: 'Here it is, so you can learn.' He never imagined what he had got into. For with the reading of Juan Rulfo I not only learned to write in a different way but always to have another story ready in order not to recount the one I'm writing. Ever since I wrote *One Hundred Years of Solitude* my absolute victim in this redemptive system has been Álvaro Mutis. For eighteen months he came to my house almost every night so I could tell him about the chapters I had completed, and in this way I caught his reactions even though they were to a different story. He listened to the chapters with so much enthusiasm that he kept repeating them everywhere, corrected and augmented by him. His friends recounted them to me afterwards, just as he had repeated them, and often I appropriated his contributions. When the first draft was finished, I sent it to his house. The next day he called me in indignation:

'You've made me look like a dog in front of my friends,' he shouted at me. 'This stuff has nothing to do with what you told me.'

Since then he has been the first reader of my manuscripts. His judgements are so severe but so well reasoned that at least three stories of mine died in the wastepaper basket because he had an argument with them. I myself couldn't say how much of him is in almost all my books, but there's a great deal.

I've often wondered how it is that this friendship has been able to prosper in such despicable times. The answer is simple: Álvaro and I see each other very little, and only as friends. Though we have lived in Mexico City for more than thirty years and are almost neighbours, that is where we see each other least. When I want to see him, or he wants to see me, we call each other first to be sure we want to see each other. I violated this elementary rule of friendship only once, and that was when Álvaro gave me an extreme demonstration of the kind of friend he is capable of being.

This is what happened: drowning in tequila, with a very dear friend, at four in the morning I knocked at the door of the apartment where Álvaro endured his sad life of a bachelor, always at one's service. Before his face still dazed by sleep, we took down a beautiful oil painting by Botero that measured 1 metre 20 by 1 metre, took it away without explanation, and did with it whatever we felt like doing. Álvaro has never said a word to me about the assault or moved a finger to find out about the painting. And I've had to wait until tonight and this celebration of his first seventy years to express my remorse to him.

Something else that has sustained this friendship is that, for the most part, when we've been together, we've been travelling. This has allowed us to be concerned with other people and other things most of the time, and to be concerned with each other when it really was worth the effort. For me, the interminable hours on European highways have been the university of arts and letters I never attended. From Barcelona to Aix-en-Provence I learned more than 300 kilometres' worth about the Cathars and the popes of Avignon. And the same thing happened in Alexandria and in Florence, in Naples and in Beirut, in Egypt and in Paris.

However, the most enigmatic instruction of

those frenzied trips happened while crossing the Belgian countryside, rarefied by October fog and the smell of human shit from recently abandoned fallow fields. Álvaro had driven for more than three hours in absolute silence, though no one believes it. Suddenly, he said: 'A country of great cyclists and hunters.' He never explained to us what he meant but confessed that inside him lives a gigantic, shaggy, drooling simpleton who, in careless moments, comes out with sentences like that one, even during the most proper visits and in presidential palaces, and that Álvaro has to keep him at arm's length when he's writing because the fool goes mad and begins to shake and stamp his feet because he wants so much to correct his books.

With it all, my best memories of that errant school haven't been the classes but the recreational periods. In Paris, waiting for our wives to finish shopping, Álvaro sat on the steps of a fashionable cafeteria, twisted his head skywards, rolled back his eyes, and extended his trembling beggar's hand. An impeccably dressed gentleman said with typical French sourness: 'It is effrontery to beg wearing a cashmere sweater like that.' But he gave him a franc. In less than fifteen minutes he had collected forty.

In Rome, in the house of Francesco Rosi, he hypnotized Fellini, Monica Vitti, Alida Valli, Alberto Moravia, the cream of Italian cinema and literature, and kept them in suspense for hours, recounting his truculent stories about Quindío in an Italian of his own invention, without knowing a single word of the language. In a bar in Barcelona he recited a poem in the languorous voice of Pablo Neruda, and someone who had heard Neruda in person asked for his autograph, thinking he was the Chilean.

A verse of his had disturbed me since the first time I read it: 'Now that I know I'll never see Istanbul'. A strange line for a hopeless monarchist who never said 'Istanbul' but 'Byzantium', just as he didn't say 'Leningrad' but 'St Petersburg' long before history sided with him. I don't know why I had the premonition that we ought to exorcize that line by seeing Istanbul. So I persuaded him that we should go there in a slow ship, as one must when defying fate. However, I didn't have a moment's peace for the three days we were there, frightened by the premonitory power of poetry. Only today, when Álvaro is an old man of seventy and I a boy of sixty-six, do I have the courage to say I didn't do it to ruin a line but to impede death.

In any event, the only time I really thought I was about to die I was also with Álvaro. We were driving across luminous Provence when a demented driver came straight at us from the opposite direction. All I could do was give the steering wheel a hard turn to the right, without having time to see where we were going to land. For a moment I had the extraordinary sensation that the wheel was not responding in empty space. Carmen and Mercedes, in the back seat as usual, were breathless until the car lay down like a child in the ditch of a springtime vineyard. All I remember of that moment is Álvaro's face in the seat beside me; he stared at me for a second before he turned away with a pitying look that seemed to say: 'But what is this asshole doing?'

These abrupt remarks of Álvaro's are less of a surprise to those of us who knew and endured his mother, Carolina Jaramillo, a beautiful, beguiling woman who did not look in the mirror again after the age of twenty because she began to see herself as different from how she felt. When she was already an elderly grandmother she travelled by bicycle, dressed as a hunter, giving free injections at farms on the savanna. In New York I asked her one night to look after my fourteen-month-old son while we went to the cinema. She warned us in all seriousness to be careful, because in Manizales she had done the same favour with a child who wouldn't stop crying, and she had been obliged to quiet him with a poisoned blackberry candy. In spite of that we entrusted him to her on another day in Macy's department store, and when we returned we found her alone. While store security looked for the boy, she tried to console us with the same dark serenity that her son had: 'Don't worry. I lost Álvarito in Brussels when he was seven, and now just see how well he's doing.' Of course he was doing well: he was an erudite, magnified version of her, and half the world knew him, not so much for his poetry as for being the most congenial man in the world. Wherever he went he left behind an unforgettable trail of his frenzied exaggerations, suicidal feasts, and ingenious fulminations. Only those of us who know and love him most know that they are no more than exaggerations to frighten away his phantoms.

No one can imagine how high a price Álvaro Mutis

pays for the misfortune of being so congenial. I have seen him lying on a sofa in the shadows of his study, with a hangover of conscience that none of his happy auditors of the previous night would envy. Fortunately, that incurable solitude is the other mother to whom he owes his immense knowledge, his enormous capacity for reading, his infinite curiosity, and the chimerical beauty and interminable desolation of his poetry.

I have seen him hidden from the world in the elephantine symphonies of Bruckner as if they were divertimentos of Scarlatti. I have seen him in an isolated corner of a garden in Cuernavaca, during a long holiday, a fugitive from reality in the enchanted forest of the complete works of Balzac. From time to time, like someone who goes to see a cowboy movie, he rereads *Remembrance of Things Past* in one sitting. A good condition for his reading a book is that it has no fewer than 1,200 pages. In the Mexico City prison where he was incarcerated for a crime that many of us writers and artists benefited from and that he alone paid for, he spent sixteen months which he considers the happiest of his life.

I always thought that the slowness of his creations was due to his tyrannical occupations. I also thought it was made worse by his disastrous handwriting, which looks as if it were made with a goose feather, by the goose himself, and whose vampirish strokes would make mastiffs howl with terror in the mists of Transylvania. When I told him this many years ago, he said that as soon as he retired from his galley slavery he would bring his books up to date. That this has happened, and that he has jumped without a parachute from his eternal aeroplanes to the firm ground of abundant, well-deserved glory, is one of the great miracles of our letters: eight books in six years.

It is enough to read a single page of any of them to understand everything: the complete works of Álvaro Mutis, his very life, are those of a seer who knows with absolute certainty that we'll never again find the paradise we have lost. That is: Maqroll is not only Mutis, as people say so easily. Maqroll is all of us.

Let those of us who have come tonight to celebrate with Álvaro these seventy years be left with this risky conclusion. For the first time with no false shyness, with no stinging insults because we're afraid to cry, let us just tell him with all our heart how much we admire him, damn it, and how much we love him.

THE ARGENTINE WHO ENDEARED HIMSELF TO EVERYBODY

Mexico City, February 12, 1994

I went to Prague for the last time, with Carlos Fuentes and Julio Cortázar, in the historic year of 1968. We were travelling by train from Paris because the three of us were united in our fear of aeroplanes, and we had talked about everything as we crossed the divided night of the Germanys, their oceans of beets, their immense factories which made everything, the devastation of their savage wars and excessive loves.

When it was time to sleep, it occurred to Carlos Fuentes to ask Cortázar how, and at what point, and by whose initiative the piano had been introduced into the jazz orchestra. The question was casual, not meant to find out more than a date and a name, but the answer was a dazzling lecture that went on until dawn, between enormous glasses of beer and icy sausages with potatoes. Cortázar, who knew how to weigh his words very carefully, offered us, with barely credible knowledge and simplicity, a historic and aesthetic review that culminated at first light in a Homeric apologia for Thelonious Monk. He spoke not only in a deep organ voice with laborious long rr's but with his big-boned hands as well, more expressive than any others I can remember. Neither Carlos Fuentes nor I will ever forget the astonishment of that incomparable night.

Twelve years later I saw Julio Cortázar in front of a crowd in a park in Managua, with no weapons other than his beautiful voice and one of his most difficult stories: the tale of a boxer down on his luck that the protagonist recounts in Lunfardo, the underworld dialect of Buenos Aires, whose comprehension would be completely forbidden to the rest of us mortals if we hadn't caught glimpses of it through so much malevolence; yet that was the story Cortázar himself chose to read on a platform in a huge illuminated garden before a crowd composed of everyone from consecrated poets and unemployed masons to *comandantes* of the revolution and their opponents. It was another dazzling experience. Although, strictly speaking, it wasn't easy to follow the sense of the story, even for the most expert in Lunfardo slang, you felt and were hurt by the blows the poor boxer received in the solitude of the ring, and his illusions and misery made you want to cry, for Cortázar had achieved so intimate a communication with his audience that no one cared any longer what the words meant or didn't mean, and the crowd sitting on the grass seemed to levitate in a state of grace because of the spell cast by a voice that didn't seem to be of this world.

These two memories of Cortázar, which affected me so much, also seem to be the ones that defined him best. They were the two extremes of his personality. In private, as on the train to Prague, he seduced with his eloquence, his lively erudition, his millimetric memory, his dangerous humour, with everything that made him one of the great intellectuals in the good sense of another time. In public,

in spite of his reluctance to be a spectacle, he fascinated the audience with an inescapable presence that
was somehow supernatural and at the same time
tender and puzzling. In both cases he was the most
remarkable human being I've had the good fortune
to know.

Years later, when we were already friends, I
thought I'd see him again as I saw him that first day,
for I think he recreated himself in one of his most
accomplished stories, 'The Other Heaven', in the
character of a Latin American in Paris who attended
executions by guillotine out of sheer curiosity. As
if he had done it in front of a mirror, Cortázar
described him in this way: 'He had at once a distant
and curiously fixed expression, the face of someone
who has become immobilized in a moment of sleep
and refuses to take the step that will return him to
wakefulness.' His character went around encased in
a long black smock, like Cortázar's own overcoat
when I saw him for the first time, but the narrator
of the story didn't dare approach to ask about his
origin, fearing the cold anger with which he himself would have received a similar question. The
strange thing is that I didn't dare approach Cortázar

either on that afternoon in the Old Navy bar, and because of the same fear. I saw him writing for more than an hour, not pausing to think, not drinking anything but half a glass of mineral water, until it began to grow dark and he put his pen in his pocket and went out, his notebook under his arm like the tallest, skinniest schoolboy in the world. On the many occasions we saw each other years later, the only thing that had changed in him was his thick, dark beard, for until two weeks before his death the legend that he was immortal seemed true, because he had never stopped growing and always stayed the age he had been when he was born. I never had the courage to ask him if it was true, as I never told him that during the sad autumn of 1956 I had seen him, without daring to say anything to him, in his corner of the Old Navy, and I know that wherever he is now he must be cursing me for my timidity. Idols fill you with respect, admiration, affection, and, of course, great envy. Cortázar inspired all those feelings as very few writers do, but he also inspired another, less frequent one: devotion. He was, perhaps unintentionally, the Argentine who endeared himself to everybody.

However, I dare to think that if the dead die, Cortázar must be dying again of embarrassment because of the worldwide consternation caused by his death. Nobody dreaded posthumous honours and funeral pomp more than he, either in real life or in books. Besides, I always thought that death itself seemed indecent to him. Somewhere in *Around the Day in Eighty Worlds*, a group of friends cannot contain their laughter at the evidence that a friend of theirs has committed the absurdity of dying. That was why, because I knew and loved him so well, I refused to take part in lamentations and elegies for Julio Cortázar.

I preferred to go on thinking of him as he undoubtedly would have wanted, with immense rejoicing that he had existed, with deep joy at having known him, and gratitude for his having left the world a body of work that may be incomplete but is as beautiful and indestructible as his memory.

LATIN AMERICA EXISTS

Contadora, Panama, March 28, 1995

I waited till the last to speak, because yesterday at breakfast I didn't know anything about what I learned during the rest of the day. I'm a diehard conversationalist and these tournaments are implacable monologues in which the pleasure of questions and replies is forbidden. You take notes, ask for the floor, wait, and when it's your turn the others have already said what you were going to say. My compatriot Augusto Ramírez had told me on the plane that it's easy to know when someone has grown old because everything he says he illustrates with an anecdote. If that's the case, I told him, I was born old and all my books are senile. These notes are proof of that.

President Lacalle gave us our first surprise with the revelation that the name of Latin America isn't French. I always thought it was, but no matter how hard I think about it, I haven't been able to remember where I learned it and, in any case, I couldn't prove it. Bolívar didn't use it. He said 'America', without adjectives, before the North Americans appropriated the name for themselves alone. But, on the other hand, Bolívar compressed into six words the chaos of our identity to define us in the Jamaica Letter: we are a "small human race". That is, he included everything left out in other definitions: our multiple origins, our indigenous languages, and the European indigenous languages – Spanish, Portuguese, English, French, Dutch.

In the 1940s the people of Amsterdam awoke to the nonsensical news that Holland was participating in a world championship of baseball – a sport foreign to the Dutch – and the fact was that Curaçao was about to win the world championship for Central America and the Caribbean. With regard to the Caribbean, I believe its area is not well defined, because it really ought to be cultural, not geographical. It ought to begin in the southern

United States and extend down to northern Brazil. Central America, which we suppose belongs to the Pacific, doesn't have much of that ocean, and its culture is Caribbean. This legitimate claim would at least have the advantage that Faulkner and all the great writers of the southern United States would begin to form part of the magical realism congregation. Also in the 1940s Giovanni Papini declared that Latin America had contributed nothing to humanity, not even a saint, as if he thought that were a small thing. He was wrong, for we already had Saint Rosa of Lima, but he didn't count her, perhaps because she was a woman. His statement illustrated very well the idea the Europeans have always had of us: everything that doesn't resemble them they think is an error, and they do everything they can to correct it in their own way, like the United States. Simón Bolívar, exasperated over so much advice and so many prescriptions, said: 'Let us have our Middle Ages in peace.'

He more than anyone endured pressure from a Europe already grown old regarding which system he ought to choose, a monarchy or a republic. A great deal has been written about his dreams of wearing a crown. The truth is, at that time, even after the North American and French revolutions, monarchy was not as anachronistic as it seems to us republicans of today. Bolívar understood it in this way and thought the system didn't matter if it served the dream of an independent, united America. That is, as he said, the largest, richest, most powerful state in the world. We were already victims of the war between dogmas that still torment us, as Sergio Ramírez reminded us yesterday: some fall and others rise, even if they are only a subterfuge, like elections in democracies.

A good example is Colombia. Regular elections are enough to legitimize the democracy, for the ritual is what matters, without worrying too much about its vices: patronage, corruption, fraud, the buying and selling of votes. Jaime Bateman, the *comandante* of the M-19, said: 'A senator isn't elected with 60,000 votes but with 60,000 pesos. Not long ago, in Cartagena, a fruit vendor shouted at me in the street: "You owe me 6,000 pesos!" The explanation is that she had voted by mistake for a candidate whose name she confused with mine, and realized it only afterwards. What could I do? I paid her the 6,000 pesos.'

The fate of the Bolívarian idea of integration seems increasingly sown with doubts, except in arts and letters, which move forward towards cultural integration on their own and at their own risk. Our dear Federico Mayor Zaragoza is right to worry about the silence of the intellectuals, but not the silence of the artists, who, after all, are not intellectuals but emotionalists. They express themselves in shouts from Río Bravo to Patagonia, in our music, our painting, our theatre and dance, our novels and soap operas. Félix B. Caignet, the father of radio soap operas, said: 'I start from the basic premise that people want to cry, and all I do is give them the excuse.' They are the simplest and richest popular expression of continental multilingualism. When political and economic integration are achieved, and they will be, cultural integration will be a long-standing, irreversible fact. Even in the United States, where enormous fortunes are spent on cultural penetration, while we, without spending a cent, are changing their language, their food, their music, their education, their styles of living and loving. That is, the most important thing in life: their culture.

One of the great joys I'll take away from these two day-long sessions with no breaks was my first meeting with my good neighbour Minister Francisco Weffort, who began by surprising us with his impeccable Spanish. And yet I wonder whether around this table there are more than two people who speak Portuguese. President de la Madrid was correct when he said that our Spanish isn't bothered by leaping across the Mato Grosso while the Brazilians, in a national effort to get along with us, are creating Portish, which may be the lingua franca of an integrated America. Pacho Weffort, as we would call him in Colombia; Pancho, as we would call him in Mexico; or Paco, as they would call him in any tavern in Spain, defends with heavyweight reasons the Ministry of Culture. I oppose, with no success, and perhaps that's fortunate, establishing one in Colombia. My principal argument is that it would contribute to the officializing and bureaucratizing of culture.

But there's no need to simplify. What I reject is

the ministerial structure, an easy victim of patronage and political manipulation. I propose instead a National Council on Culture that would not be governmental but part of the state, responsible to the president of the republic and not to Congress, and safe from frequent ministerial crises, palace intrigues, and the black arts of the budget. Thanks to Pacho's excellent Spanish, and in spite of my embarrassing Portish, we have agreed that it doesn't matter how it's done as long as the state assumes the grave responsibility of preserving and extending the cultural sphere.

President de la Madrid did us the great favour of bringing up the drama of drug trafficking. For him, the United States every day supplies between 20 and 30 million drug addicts with no difficulty at all, almost providing home delivery of drugs as if they were milk, the newspaper, or bread. This is possible only with mafias stronger than the Colombian, and greater corruption among the authorities than in Colombia. The problem of narcotraffic of course touches us Colombians very deeply. By now we're almost the only ones responsible for narcotraffic, the only ones responsible for the United States having that great consumers' market, which, sad to say, makes the narcotraffic industry so prosperous in Colombia. My impression is that the traffic in drugs is a problem that has slipped out of humanity's hands. This doesn't mean we should be pessimists and declare ourselves defeated, but we must continue to combat the problem starting from that point of view and not from the starting point of fumigation.

Not long ago I was with a group of North American reporters on a small plateau that couldn't have had more than three or four hectares planted in poppies. We were given a demonstration: fumigation from helicopters, fumigation from planes. By the third pass of helicopters and planes we calculated that this probably cost more than the plot of land. It's disheartening to know that this in no way will combat drug trafficking. I told some of the North American reporters who were with us that fumigation ought to begin with the island of Manhattan and the city hall of Washington. I reproached them, too, because they and the rest of the world know about the drugs in Colombia – how it is planted, how it is processed, how it is exported –

because we Colombian journalists have investigated it, published it, made it known throughout the world. Many have even paid with their lives. On the other hand, no North American journalist has taken the trouble to tell us how drugs enter the United States and what their internal distribution and commercialization are like.

I believe we all eventually agreed with the conclusion of former president Lacalle that the redemption of these Americas lies in education. We arrived at the same conclusion last year at UNESCO's Forum for Reflection, where the beautiful idea of a 'long-distance university' was outlined. There it fell to me once again to uphold the idea of an early apprehension of the aptitudes and vocations that the world needs so much. The basis of it is that if a child is placed in front of a group of different toys, he or she will eventually keep just one, and the duty of the state would be to create the conditions for that toy remaining with that child. I am convinced this is the secret formula for happiness and longevity. That each person can live and do only what he or she likes, from the cradle to the grave. At the same time, we all agree, apparently, that we must be alert to the tendency of the state to disengage from education and entrust it to private entities. The argument against this is devastating: private education, good or bad, is the most effective form of social discrimination.

A good ending for a four-hour relay race, which can serve to dissipate doubts regarding whether Latin America really exists, is that from the beginning former president Lacalle and Augusto Ramírez hurled at this table a kind of fragmentation grenade. Well, to judge by what has been said here during these two days, there is not the slightest doubt that it exists. Perhaps its Oedipal destiny is to continue searching for its identity for ever, which will be a creative fate that would make us distinctive in the world's eyes. Battered and dispersed, still incomplete, and always searching for an ethic of life, Latin America exists. The proof? In these two days we've had it: we think, therefore we exist.

A DIFFERENT NATURE IN A WORLD DIFFERENT FROM OURS

Santafé de Bogotá, Colombia, April 12, 1996

I heard about the military for the first time at a very early age, when my grandfather told me a blood-curdling tale about what used to be called the Banana massacre. That is: the repression by gunfire of a demonstration by Colombians working for the United Fruit Company who were cornered in the Ciénaga railway station. My grandfather, a silver-smith by trade and a diehard liberal, had been promoted to colonel in the ranks of General Rafael Uribe Uribe during the Thousand Days' War, and because of that distinction had been present at the signing of the Treaty of Neerlandia, which ended half a century of formal civil wars. Facing him on the other side of the table was his oldest son, a conservative parliamentarian.

I believe my vision of the drama of the banana workers as recounted by him was the most intense of my early years, and also the most enduring, to the extent that I remember it now as a subject that obsessed my family and their friends throughout my childhood and somehow conditioned our lives forever. But it also had an enormous historical importance, because it precipitated the end of more than forty years of hegemonies and undoubtedly influenced the subsequent organization of the military profession.

But it marked me forever for another reason that is relevant now: it was the first image I had of the military, and many years would go by before I not only began to change it but also to reduce it to reasonable proportions. In reality, in spite of my conscious efforts to exorcize it, in fifty years I've never had the opportunity to converse with more than half a dozen military men, and I managed to be spontaneous and unguarded with very few. The impression of mutual uncertainties always hampered our encounters, I never could overcome the idea that words didn't mean the same thing for them as for me, and that in the long run we didn't have anything to talk about.

You shouldn't think I was indifferent to the problem. On the contrary: it is one of my great frustrations. I also wondered where the fault lay, in the military or in me, and how it would be possible to demolish that bastion of non-communication. It wouldn't be easy. During the first two years of studying law at the Universidad Nacional — when I was nineteen — two of my classmates were lieutenants in the army. (I really wish they were here among you.) They came to class in their identical, impeccable uniforms, always together and always punctual. They sat to one side and were the most serious and methodical students, but it always seemed to me that they were in a world different from ours. If you spoke to them, they were attentive and pleasant, but invincibly formal: they replied only to what they had been asked. At exam time we civilians divided into groups of four to study in cafés, we'd see one another at the Saturday dances, at student rock-throwing fights, in the tame taverns and lugubrious brothels of the period, but we never ran into our military classmates, not even by accident.

It was impossible not to conclude that their nature was different. In general, the children of military men are military men, they live in their own neighbourhoods, meet in their casinos and clubs, and their worlds go by behind closed doors. It wasn't easy to find them in the cafés, rarely at the cinema, and they had a mysterious aura that made them recognizable even in civilian clothes. The very nature of their work has made them nomads, and this has given them the opportunity to know even the farthest corners of the country, on the inside and the outside, but by their own choice they do not have the right to vote. Out of elementary good manners, I have learned I don't know how many times to recognize their insignias in order not to make a mistake when I greet them, and it has taken me longer to learn this than to forget it.

Some friends familiar with my prejudices think this visit is the strangest thing I've ever done. But my obsession with different forms of power is more than literary – it is almost anthropological – ever since my grandfather told me about the tragedy in Ciénaga. I've often wondered whether that isn't the origin of a thematic line that runs through the centre of all my books. In *Leaf Storm*, which is the convalescence of the town after the exodus of the banana growers; in the colonel nobody wrote to in *In Evil Hour*, which is a reflection on the use of the military for a political cause; in Colonel Aureliano Buendía, who wrote verses in the clamour of his thirty-two wars; and in the patriarch more than two hundred years old who never learned to write. From the first to the last of these books – and I hope in many others in the future – there is a whole lifetime of questions about the nature of power.

I believe that my real awareness of all this began when I was writing *One Hundred Years of Solitude*. What most inspired me then was the possibility of a historical vindication for the victims of the tragedy, as opposed to the official history that proclaimed it a victory for law and order. But it was impossible: I couldn't find any direct or remote evidence that the dead had numbered more than seven and that the extent of the drama hadn't been the one wandering through collective memory. Which, of course, did not diminish in any way the magnitude of the catastrophe, given the size of the country.

You might ask, and with reason, why, instead of recounting it in its real proportions, I magnified it to three thousand dead who were transported in a train two hundred carriages long and thrown into the sea. The reason, in poetic code, is simple: I was working in a dimension where the episode of the banana workers was no longer a historical horror from nowhere but an event of mythic proportions in which the victims were not the same and the executioners no longer had faces and names, and perhaps no one was innocent. From that lack of restraint the old patriarch came to me, dragging his solitary hernia through a palace filled with cows.

How could it be otherwise? The only mythical creature Latin America has produced is the military dictator from the end of the last century and the beginning of this one. Many of them, it is true, liberal caudillos who in the end turned into savage tyrants. I'm convinced that if Colonel Aureliano Buendía had won even one of his thirty-two wars, he would have been one of them.

However, when I fulfilled the dream of writing about the last days of the Liberator, Simón Bolívar, in *The General in His Labyrinth*, I had to twist the neck of the swan of invention. This was a flesh-and-blood man of extraordinary stature who waged war against his devastated body with no witnesses other than the entourage of young soldiers who accompanied him in all his wars and would accompany him till death. I had to know how he really was, and how each of them was, and I believe I discovered this as much as possible in the Liberator's revealing, fascinating letters. I believe, in all humility, that *The General in His Labyrinth* is historic testimony wrapped in the irresistible trappings of poetry.

It is about these literary enigmas that I would like to continue the dialogue with you that other friends have begun during the past few days. Those who have applauded the military branch know I'm no stranger to that necessary idea, and my one hope is that it prospers. Each one has talked about his speciality. I have none except letters, and even here I'm an empiricist with no academic formation, but I do feel able to enrol you in the not always peaceful armies of literature. To begin with, I want to leave you with just one sentence: 'I believe all our lives would be better if each of you would always carry a book in your knapsack.'

JOURNALISM: THE BEST JOB IN THE WORLD

Los Angeles, United States, October 7, 1996

A Colombian university was asked what aptitude and vocational tests they give to those who want to study journalism, and the response was categorical: 'Journalists are not artists.' These reflections, on the contrary, are based precisely on the certainty that written journalism is a literary genre.

Some fifty years ago, schools of journalism were not the fashion. One learned in editorial rooms, printing plants, the little café across the street, the Friday drinking sessions. The entire newspaper was a factory that formed and informed without equivocation and generated opinion in a participatory atmosphere that kept morality in its place. For we journalists always went around together, lived together, and were such occupational fanatics that we didn't talk about anything else but the job. The work brought with it a group friendship that left little room for a private life. Institutional editorial meetings did not exist but, at five in the afternoon, with no official notification, the entire staff took a break from the tensions of the day and assembled to have coffee somewhere in the editorial offices. It was an open meeting where topics from each section were discussed in a heated way and final touches given to the morning edition. Those who didn't learn in those twenty-four-hours-a-day ambulatory and impassioned lecture halls, or became bored by talking so much about the same thing, wanted to be or thought they were journalists but really weren't.

In those days the paper divided into three large sections: news, feature articles and special reports, and editorial notes. The most difficult and prestigious was editorial. The most inauspicious position was that of reporter, which suggested both an apprentice and a hod carrier. Time and the job itself have shown that the nervous system of journalism in fact circulates counterclockwise. I can confirm this: at the age of nineteen – being the worst student in law school – I began my career subediting editorial notes and, little by little, by working very hard, I climbed ladders in the different sections until I reached the highest rung of common reporter.

Just doing the job imposed the need for developing a cultural foundation, and the atmosphere of the job took care of fostering it. Reading was an occupational addiction. Autodidacts tend to be avid, fast readers, and those of us from that time carried those tendencies to extremes in order to keep making our way in life towards the best job in the world, as we ourselves called it. Alberto Lleras Camargo, who was always a journalist, and president of Colombia twice, didn't even have a secondary-school diploma.

The subsequent creation of schools of journalism was a pedagogical reaction to the accomplished fact that the job lacked academic endorsement. Now they're no longer just for the written press, but for all media invented and still to be invented.

Yet in their expansion they took away even the humble name the job has had since its origins in the fifteenth century, and now it's called not journalism but communication sciences or social communication. The result, in general, isn't encouraging. The young people who leave the academies full of dreams, their lives ahead of them, seem disconnected from reality and its vital problems, and a zeal for prominence takes priority over one's vocation and innate aptitudes. And over the two most important qualifications in particular: creativity and skill.

Most graduates arrive with flagrant deficiencies: they have serious problems in grammar and spelling and difficulties in having a responsive understanding of texts. Some boast that they can read a secret document on a minister's desk upside down, record casual conversations without the other person's knowledge, or make use in an article of a conversation they had agreed would be confidential. The most serious issue is that these ethical violations obey an audacious notion of the job, consciously adopted and proudly based on the sanctification of being first at any cost and above all else. Some graduates are not moved by the basic principle that the superior news article isn't always the first one turned in but is often the best one. Some, aware of their deficiencies, feel cheated by school and do not hesitate to blame their teachers for not having inculcated the virtues that are now demanded of them, in particular a curiosity about life.

It is true that these criticisms hold for education in general, perverted by the 'massification' of schools that follow the debased policy of informing instead of forming. But in the specific case of journalism, it also seems that the job didn't manage to evolve at the same speed as its tools, and journalists became lost in the labyrinth of a technology hurtling without control into the future. In other words, companies have engaged wholeheartedly in a fierce competition for material modernization and have left for later the formation of their foot soldiers and the participatory procedures that strengthened a professional spirit in the past. Editorial rooms are aseptic laboratories for solitary navigators, where it seems easier to communicate with the phenomena of space than with the hearts of readers. Dehumanization runs amok.

It isn't easy to understand that the technological splendour and communications vertigo that we longed for in our day have only anticipated and worsened the daily agony of press time. Beginners complain that editors allow three hours for a job that at the moment of truth is impossible in less than six, order them to write enough material for two columns and at the hour of truth assign them only half a column, and in the panic of press time, no one has the time or inclination to explain why, let alone offer a word of consolation. 'They don't even curse at us,' says a novice reporter yearning for direct communication with his superiors. Nothing: the editor who once had been a wise, compassionate father barely has the energy and time himself to survive the galley slavery of technology.

I believe it is undue haste and space limitations that have minimized feature writing, which we always considered the star genre, but it is also the one that requires more time, more research, more reflection, and a sure knowledge of the art of writing. It is, in fact, the meticulous, truthful reconstitution of an event. In other words: the complete news item, just as it really happened, so that the reader knows it as well as if he'd been there, in the place where the events occurred.

Before the teletype and the telex were invented, a radio operator with a martyr's vocation captured in mid-flight the news of the world in sidereal whistles, and an erudite subeditor completed them with details and antecedents, just as the entire skeleton of a dinosaur is reconstructed on the basis of a single vertebra. Only interpretation was forbidden, because that was the sacred domain of the managing editor, whose editorials, it was assumed, were written out by him, even if they weren't, and almost always in a hand famous for its inscrutability. Historic managing editors had personal linotypists to decipher them.

An important advance over this half-century is that now there is commentary and opinion in news articles and feature writing, and editorials are enriched with informative data. The results, however, don't appear to be the very best, for this profession has never been as dangerous as it is now. The excessive use of quotations and false or true statements permits innocent or deliberate mistakes, vicious manipulations, and venomous misrepresentations that give the news article the dimensions of a deadly weapon. Citations of sources that deserve full credit, of generally well-informed people, or high-placed officials who requested anonymity, or observers who know everything and whom no one sees, shelter all kinds of offences that go unpunished. But the one responsible takes refuge in the right not to reveal his source, not asking whether he himself isn't an easy tool of the source who passed on information however he chose, arranged however it suited him best.

I think he is: the bad journalist thinks the source is his very life – above all, if it is official – and for that reason he sanctifies it, pampers it, protects it, and eventually establishes a dangerous complicit relationship that even leads him to underrate the integrity of a second source.

Even at the risk of being too anecdotal, I believe there is another guilty party in this drama: the tape recorder. Before it was invented, the profession got along very well with three tools that really were only one: a notebook, unswerving ethics, and two ears that we reporters still used to hear what people said to us. The professional, ethical management of the tape recorder has not yet been invented. Someone would have to teach our young colleagues that the cassette isn't a substitute for memory but a development of the humble notebook that gave such good service in the early days of the job. The tape recorder hears but doesn't listen, it repeats – like a digital parrot – but doesn't think, is faithful but has no heart, and, in the long run, its literal version will not be as trustworthy as that of somebody who pays attention to the living words of his interlocutor, evaluates them with his intelligence, and assesses them with his morality. For the radio it has the enormous advantage of literalness and immediacy, but many interviewers don't listen to the answers because they're thinking about the next question.

The tape recorder is responsible for the relentless expansion of the interview. Radio and television, by their very nature, transformed it into the supreme genre, but the written press also seems to share the mistaken idea that the voice of truth is not so much that of the journalist who has seen as that of the interviewee who has stated. For many subeditors on newspapers, transcription is the trial by fire: they confuse the sound of words, stumble over semantics, founder on the rocks of spelling, and die of an infarction of syntax. Perhaps the solution is to return to the poor notebook so that the journalist keeps editing with his intelligence as he listens, and leave the tape recorder to its true position as invaluable witness. In any case, it is a consolation to suppose that many of the ethical and other transgressions that debase and embarrass today's journalism are not always because of immorality but are also due to a lack of professional mastery.

Perhaps the misfortune of the schools of social communication is that they teach many things useful to the job but very little about the job itself. Of course, they ought to continue with their humanities programmes, but make them less ambitious and peremptory, in order to contribute to the cultural base the students don't bring with them from secondary school. But all the training should rest on three central pillars: the priority of aptitudes and vocations, the certainty that investigation is not a professional speciality but that all journalism should, by definition, be investigative, and the awareness that ethics are not an occasional condition but should always accompany journalism like the buzz accompanies the blowfly.

The final objective should be a return to the primary system of teaching journalism by means of practical workshops in small groups, making critical use of historical experience within its original frame of public service. In other words: rescuing for apprentices the spirit of the five o'clock get-together.

We, a group of independent journalists, are trying to do this for all of Latin America from Cartagena de Indias, with a system of experimental, travelling workshops that bears the immodest name of Foundation for a New Ibero-American Journalism. It is a pilot experiment in which new journalists work on a particular speciality – feature writing, editing, radio and television interviews, and many others – under the direction of a veteran reporter.

In response to a public announcement by the foundation, candidates are proposed by the medium in which they work, which is responsible for the costs of their travel, lodging, and fees. They should be younger than thirty, have a minimum of three years' experience, and vouch for their aptitude in and degree of knowledge of their speciality with samples that they themselves consider their best and worst work. The duration of each workshop depends on the availability of the invited instructor – which rarely can be more than a week – who does not attempt to instruct the participants with theoretical dogmas and academic prejudices but to strengthen them at the round table by means of practical exercises, attempting to pass on his or her experiences in the carpentry of the job. For the purpose is not to teach them to be journalists but to improve through practice those who already are. There are no final examinations or evaluations, and no diplomas or certificates of any kind are issued: life will take care of deciding who is suitable and who is not.

Three hundred and twenty young journalists from eleven countries have participated in twenty-seven workshops in only a year and a half since the creation of the foundation, led by veterans of ten nationalities. Alma Guillermoprieto inaugurated the project with two workshops on feature writing and reporting. Terry Anderson led another on information in dangerous situations, with the cooperation of a general of the armed forces, who pointed out very clearly the line between heroism and suicide. Tomás Eloy Martínez, our most faithful and combative collaborator, gave a workshop on editing and then another on journalism in times of crisis. Phil Bennett gave his on tendencies of the press in the United

States, and Stephen Ferry did his on photography. The magnificent Horacio Verbitsky and the meticulous Tim Golden explored different areas of investigative journalism, and the Spaniard Miguel Ángel Bastenier led a seminar on international journalism and fascinated the participants with a brilliant critical analysis of the European press.

One workshop between managing editors and subeditors had very positive results, and next year we dream of convening a massive exchange of Sunday edition experiences among editors from all around the world. I myself have succumbed several times to the temptation of persuading workshop participants that an authoritative feature can ennoble the press with translucent nuggets of poetry.

The benefits garnered so far are not easy to evaluate from a pedagogical point of view, but we take as encouraging symptoms the growing enthusiasm of the workshop participants, who are already a swelling leaven of non-conformity and creative subversion within their media, shared in many cases with their management. The mere fact of arranging for twenty journalists from different countries to meet and talk for five days about the job is an achievement for them and for the job. For, in the long run, we are not proposing a new way of teaching journalism but trying to reinvent the old way of learning it.

The media would do well to support this rescue operation, whether in their editorial rooms or with intentionally constructed scenarios, like simulators that reproduce all the incidents of a flight so that students learn to avoid disasters before encountering them in real life. For journalism is an insatiable passion that can only be endured and humanized by its naked confrontation with reality. No one who has not suffered it can imagine this servitude that feeds on the unexpected in life. No one who has not experienced it can even conceive of the supernatural throbbing of the news, the orgasm of breaking a story, the moral devastation of failure. No one who has not been born for it and is not prepared to live for it alone could continue in so incomprehensible and voracious a job, whose work ends after each news report as if it were forever but that does not grant a moment's peace until in the next minute it begins all over again more ardently than before.

A BOTTLE IN THE OCEAN
FOR THE GOD OF WORDS

Zacatecas, Mexico, April 7, 1997

When I was twelve I was almost run down by a
bicycle. A passing priest saved me with a shout:
'Watch out!' The cyclist fell to the ground. The
priest, without stopping, said to me: 'Now do you
see the power of the word?' That day I found out.
Now we also know that the Maya peoples had
known it since the time of Christ, and with so much
precision that they had a special god of words.

That power has never been as great as it is today.
Humanity will enter the third millennium under
the sway of words. It isn't true that the image is dis-
placing them or can annihilate them. On the
contrary, it is empowering them: there have never

been so many words in the world with so much scope, authority, and volition as in the immense Babel of life today. Words invented, mistreated, or sanctified by the press, by throw-away books, by advertising posters: spoken and sung on the radio, on television, in films, on the phone, on loudspeakers; shouted with a broad brush on the walls of buildings or whispered in the ear in the penumbra of love. No, what has been routed is silence. Things now have so many names in so many languages that it is no longer easy to know what they are called in any of them. Languages scatter, out of control, they mingle and mix together, dashing blindly towards the ineluctable destiny of a global vernacular.

The Spanish language has to be prepared for a great cycle in that future without frontiers. It is a historical right. Not because of its economic influence, like other languages until today, but because of its vitality, its creative dynamism, its vast cultural experience, the rapidity and strength of its expansion in its own sphere of 19 million square kilometres and 400 million speakers by the end of the century. A teacher of Hispanic literature in the United States has said, and with reason, that his time in class is spent serving as an interpreter for Latin Americans from different countries. It is surprising that the verb *pasar* has fifty-four meanings, while in the Republic of Ecuador the male sexual organ has 105 names but the word *condoliente*, which is self-explanatory and which we have so much need of, has not yet been invented. A young French journalist is overwhelmed by the poetic discoveries he finds everywhere in our domestic life. That a child, kept awake by the sad, intermittent bleat of a lamb, said: 'It sounds like a lighthouse.' That a food seller in Colombian Guajira turned down a brew of lemon balm because it tasted of Good Friday. That Don Sebastián de Covarrubias, in his memorable dictionary, wrote for us in his own hand that yellow is the colour of lovers. How many times haven't we had coffee that tastes of window, bread that tastes of corner, cherries that taste of kiss? These are positive proofs of the intelligence of a language that for some time has been bursting at the seams. Yet our contribution should not be controlling it but, on the contrary, freeing it from its normative shackles so that it can enter the twenty-first century as if it owned the place.

In that sense, I would dare to suggest to this learned audience that we simplify grammar before grammar ends up simplifying us. Let us humanize its rules, let us learn from the indigenous languages to which we owe so much and that still have a great deal with which to teach and enrich us, let us assimilate quickly and thoroughly technical and scientific neologisms before they seep in undigested, let us negotiate wholeheartedly with barbaric gerunds, endemic *thats*, the parasitic *ofwhichism*, and return to the present subjunctive the splendour of its anapaests: *váyamos* instead of *vayamos*, *cántemos* instead of *cantemos*, or the harmonious *muéramos* instead of the sinister *muramos*. Let us retire orthography, the terror of human beings from the cradle: let us bury the H written on the walls of caves, sign a boundary treaty between G and J, and be more rational about written accent marks, since, after all, no one is going to read *lagrima* [he cries] where it says *lágrima* [tear], or confuse *revolver* [to turn over] with *revólver* [revolver]. And what about our *b-burro* and our *v-vaca*, which our Spanish grandparents brought to us as if they were two when there's always one too many?

These are random questions, of course, like bottles thrown into the sea in the hope they reach the god of words. Unless, because of these audacious and foolish words, he and all of us end up lamenting, with reason and fairness, that the providential bicycle when I was twelve didn't run me down in time.

DREAMS FOR THE
TWENTY-FIRST CENTURY

Paris, France, March 8, 1999

The Italian writer Giovanni Papini infuriated our grandparents in the 1940s with a venomous sentence: 'America is made from the waste of Europe.' Today we not only have reasons to suspect that it is true, but also something even sadder: that the fault is ours.

Simón Bolívar had foreseen this and wanted to create for us an awareness of our own identity in the brilliant line from his Jamaica Letter: 'We are a small human race.' He dreamed, and said as much, that we would be the largest, most powerful, most united country on earth. At the end of his days, mortified by a debt to the English that we still haven't paid in full, and tormented by the French who were trying to sell him the last bits and pieces of their revolution, he pleaded in exasperation: 'Let us have our Middle Ages in peace.' We ended up being a laboratory of failed dreams. Our greatest virtue is creativity, and yet we have not done much more than survive on reheated doctrines and other people's wars, heirs of an unfortunate Christopher Columbus who found us by accident when he was looking for the Indies.

Not many years ago it was easier to know us among ourselves in the Latin Quarter in Paris than in any of our countries. In the small cafés of Saint-Germain-des-Prés we traded serenades from Chapultepec for gusts of wind from Comodoro Rivadavia, stewed conger eel from Pablo Neruda for twilights from the Caribbean, nostalgia for an idyllic, remote world where we had been born without even asking ourselves who we were. Today, as we see, nobody has thought it strange that we had to cross the vast Atlantic to find ourselves in Paris with ourselves.

It is your task, you dreamers younger than forty, to resolve these immense injustices. Remember that the things of this world, from heart transplants to Beethoven's quartets, were in the minds of their creators before they existed in reality. Don't expect anything from the twenty-first century, for it's the twenty-first century that expects everything from you. A century that doesn't come factory-made but ready to be forged by you in our image and likeness, and that will be only as peaceful and as much our own as you are capable of imagining it.

THE BELOVED THOUGH
DISTANT HOMELAND

Medellín, Colombia, May 18, 2003

'All these squalls to which we have been subjected are signs that the weather will soon improve and things will go well for us, because it is not possible for the bad or the good to endure for ever, and from this it follows that since the bad has lasted so long a time, the good is close at hand.'

This beautiful sentence by Don Miguel de Cervantes Saavedra does not refer to the Colombia of today but to his own time, of course, but in beginning this lament, he never would have dreamed it would fit us like a glove. For a ghostly synthesis of what contemporary Colombia is does not allow one to believe that Don Miguel would have said what he said, and said it so beautifully, if he had been a compatriot of ours. Two examples would have been enough to destroy his illusions: last year, close to 400,000 Colombians had to flee their houses and land because of the violence, as almost 3 million others had already done for the same reason over the previous half-century. These displacements were the embryo of another rootless country — almost as populous as Bogotá, and perhaps larger than Medellín — that wanders aimlessly within its own sphere, searching for a place to survive, with no more material wealth than the clothes on its back. The paradox is that these fugitives from themselves continue to be victims of the violence sustained by two of the most sustainable businesses in this irrational world: drug trafficking and the illegal sale of weapons.

They are primary symptoms of the groundswell that is suffocating Colombia: two countries in one, not only different but opposites in the colossal black market that sustains the drug trade in the United States and Europe and, in the long run, the entire world. For it is impossible to imagine the end of violence in Colombia without the elimination of narcotraffic, and the end of narcotraffic is unimaginable without the legalization of drugs, which become more profitable the more they are prohibited.

Four decades of every conceivable disturbance of public order have absorbed more than a generation of the marginalized with no way to live other than subversion or common criminality. The writer R. H. Moreno Durán said it with greater accuracy: 'Without death, Colombia would give no signs of life.' We are born suspicious and die guilty. For years, peace talks – with minimal but memorable exceptions – have ended in blood talks. For any international matter, from innocent tourist travel to the simple act of buying or selling, we Colombians have to begin by demonstrating our innocence.

In any case, the political and social atmosphere was never conducive to the peaceful homeland our grandparents dreamed of. It succumbed early to a system of inequalities, to a confessional education, a rockbound feudalism, and a deep-rooted centralism, with a remote, self-absorbed capital in the clouds and two eternal parties, at once enemies and accomplices, bloody, crooked elections, and an entire saga of governments without a people. So much ambition could be sustained only by twenty-nine civil wars and three military coups between the two parties, in a social broth that seemed anticipated by the devil for today's misfortunes in an oppressed nation that in the midst of so many misfortunes has learned to be happy without happiness, and even in spite of it.

And so we have reached a point that barely allows us to survive, but there are still some puerile souls who look to the United States as a polestar of salvation with the certainty that in our country we have used up even the sighs to die in peace. However, what they find there is a blind empire that no longer considers Colombia a good neighbour, or even a cheap, trustworthy accomplice, but only another target for its imperial voracity.

Two natural gifts have helped us avoid the empty spaces in our cultural predicament, grope for an identity, and find the truth in the fogs of uncertainty. One is the gift of creativity. The other is a raging personal determination to move up. From our very origins, both virtues nourished the natives' providential shrewdness which was used against the Spanish from the day they disembarked. The conquerors, dazzled by novels of chivalry, were beguiled by dreams of fantastic cities built of pure gold or the legend of a king covered in gold swimming in lagoons of emeralds. Masterpieces of a creative imagination intensified by magical means to survive the invader.

Some 5 million Colombians who live abroad today, fleeing from native misfortunes with no other weapons or shields than their temerity or ingenuity, have demonstrated that this prehistoric cunning is still alive in us, allowing us to survive by hook or by crook. The virtue that saves us is that, by the grace and works of our creative imaginations, we do not allow ourselves to die of hunger, for we have known how to be fakirs in India, English teachers in New York, or camel drivers in the Sahara. As I have tried to show in some of my books – if not in all of them – I trust more in these absurdities of reality than in theoretical dreams that most of the time serve only to muzzle a bad conscience. That is why I believe we still have a deeper country to discover in the midst of disaster: a secret Colombia that no longer fits in the moulds we had forged for ourselves with our historical follies.

It is not, therefore, surprising that we should begin to glimpse an apotheosis of artistic creativity among Colombians and to effect the country's good health with a definitive awareness of who we are and what we're good for. I believe Colombia is learning to survive with an indestructible faith, whose greatest merit is being more fruitful the more it encounters adversity. Historical violence forced it to decentralize, but it can still reunite with its own greatness through the work and grace of its misfortunes. Experiencing that miracle in the deepest way will allow us to know with certainty and forever in what country we were born and to continue between two opposing realities without dying. This is why I am not surprised that, in these days of historical disasters, the good health of the country should prosper with a new awareness. Popular wisdom is making its way, and we aren't waiting for it sitting in the doorway of the house but in the middle of the street, perhaps without the country itself realizing that we are going to overcome everything and find its salvation even where it had never been sought before.

No occasion seemed more auspicious than this

one for me to leave the eternal, nostalgic clandestinity of my study and stitch together these ramblings for the two hundredth anniversary of the University of Antioquia, which we celebrate now as a historical date that belongs to everyone. An auspicious occasion to begin again at the beginning and love as never before the country we deserve so that it will deserve us. If only for that reason, I would dare to believe that the dream of Don Miguel de Cervantes is now at the right point for us to glimpse the dawn of a calmer time, that the evil that overwhelms us will last much less time than the good, and that on our boundless creativity alone depends knowing now which of the many roads are the right ones, in order to experience them in the peace of the living and enjoy them by right and for ever more.

Amen.

A SOUL OPEN TO BE FILLED WITH MESSAGES IN SPANISH

Cartagena de Indias, Colombia, March 26, 2007

Not even in my most delirious dreams in the days when I was writing *One Hundred Years of Solitude* did I imagine I would see an edition of 1 million copies. To think that a million people could decide to read something written in the solitude of a room, with only the twenty-eight letters of the Spanish alphabet and two fingers as the entire arsenal, seemed madness from every point of view. Today, the Academies of the Language have published this edition as a gesture towards a novel that has passed before the eyes of fifty times a million readers, and towards an insomniac artisan like me, who cannot leave behind his surprise at everything that has happened.

But this is not and cannot be a matter of honouring a writer. This miracle is the irrefutable demonstration that there are an enormous number of people prepared to read stories in the Spanish language, and therefore a million copies of *One Hundred Years of Solitude* are not a million tributes to the writer who blushes as he receives today the first book of this print run. It is proof that there are millions of readers of texts in the Spanish language waiting for this nourishment.

Nothing has changed since then in my writing routine. I have never seen anything other than my two index fingers striking one by one and at a brisk pace the twenty-eight letters of the unmodified alphabet that I've had before my eyes for more than seventy years. Today, it was incumbent upon me to lift my head and attend this tribute, for which I am grateful, and all I can do is stop and think about what it is that has happened. What I see is that the non-existent reader of my blank page is today an immense crowd hungry to read texts in Spanish.

The readers of *One Hundred Years of Solitude* are a community who, if they lived on the same piece of ground, would be one of the twenty most popu-lous countries in the world. This isn't a boastful statement. Just the opposite. I simply want to show that there are a number of human beings who have demonstrated with their habit of reading that their souls are open to be filled with messages in Spanish. The challenge for all writers, all the poets, narra-tors, and educators in our language, is to quench that thirst and increase that crowd, the real *raison d'être* of our craft and, of course, ourselves.

When I was thirty-eight, having already pub-lished four books since my twenties, I sat down at the typewriter and wrote: 'Many years later, as he faced the firing squad, Colonel Aureliano Buendía was to remember that distant afternoon when his father took him to discover ice.' I had no idea of the significance or the origin of that sentence, or of where it would lead me. What I know today is that for eighteen months I didn't stop writing for a sin-gle day until I finished the book.

It may seem untrue, but one of my most pressing problems was typewriter paper. I was ignorant enough to think that mistakes in typing, language, or grammar were actually creative errors, and whenever I found them I tore up the page and tossed it in the wastepaper basket to start again. With the rhythm I had acquired in a year of practice, I calculated it would take me six months of daily mornings to finish the book.

Esperanza Araiza, the unforgettable Pera, the typist for poets and filmmakers, had typed fair copies of great works by Mexican writers. Among them, Carlos Fuentes' *Where the Air is Clear*, Juan Rulfo's *Pedro Páramo*, and several original scripts by Don Luis Buñuel. When I proposed that she type up the final version, the novel was a rough draft riddled with corrections, first in black ink and then in red to avoid confusion. But that was nothing for a woman accustomed to everything in a lion's cage. Years later, Pera confessed that, as she was taking home the final version that I had corrected, she slipped as she got off the bus in torrential rain, and the pages were left floating in the quagmire of the street. She gathered them, soaking wet and almost illegible, with the help of other passengers, and dried them in her house, page by page, with an iron.

What could have been the inspiration for another, better book was how Mercedes and I survived with our two sons during that time when I didn't earn a penny anywhere. I don't even know how Mercedes managed to have food in the house every day during those months. We had resisted the temptation of loans with interest until we tied up our hearts and made our first incursions into the pawnshop.

After the short-lived relief afforded by certain small things, we had to turn to the jewellery that Mercedes had received from her family over the years. The expert examined them with the rigour of a surgeon, inspected and checked again with his magical eye the diamonds in the earrings, the emeralds in the necklace, the rubies in the rings, and finally returned them to us with the long *verónica* of a bullfighter: 'All of this is nothing but glass.'

In the moments of greatest difficulty, Mercedes made her astral calculations and told the patient landlord, without the slightest tremor in her voice:

'We can pay you the full amount in six months.'

'Excuse me, señora,' the owner replied, 'but do you realize that by then it will be an enormous amount?'

'I do realize that,' said an impassive Mercedes, 'but by then we'll have everything resolved. Don't worry.'

And when she responded to the good lawyer who was a highly placed state official and one of the most elegant and patient men we had ever met, again her voice didn't tremble:

'Very well, señora, your word is good enough for me,' and he made his fatal calculations. 'I'll expect you on September 7.'

At last, at the beginning of August 1966, Mercedes and I went to the post office in Mexico City to send to Buenos Aires the finished version of *One Hundred Years of Solitude*, a package containing 590 pages typed double spaced on ordinary paper, and addressed to Francisco Porrúa, literary director of Editorial Sudamericana.

The post-office clerk placed the package on the scale, made his mental calculations, and said:

'That'll be eighty-two pesos.'

Mercedes counted the notes and loose change remaining in her purse and confronted reality.

'We have only fifty-three.'

We opened the package, divided it in half, and sent one to Buenos Aires without even asking ourselves how we would get the money to post the rest. Only afterwards did we realize that we hadn't sent the first half but the second. But before we got hold of the money to mail it, Paco Porrúa, our man in Editorial Sudamericana, anxious to read the first half of the book, forwarded us the money so that we could send it to him.

That was how we were reborn into our new life of today.

EDITOR'S NOTE

The texts that Gabriel García Márquez has brought together in this book were written by the author, intended to be read by him in public before an audience, and cover practically his entire life, from the first one, which he wrote at the age of seventeen to say goodbye to his classmates in the advanced course in Zipaquirá, in 1944, to the one he read before the Academies of the Language and the king and queen of Spain in 2007.

In the earliest texts the aversion the young Colombian feels towards oratory is explicit. 'I'm not here to give a speech' is the warning he gives his secondary-school friends the first time he stands at the podium, and the phrase our author chose as the title of this book. In the following text, 'How I Began to Write', read when he was already the successful author of One Hundred Years of Solitude, *in 1970, he again informs his listeners of his aversion to the genre: 'I began to be a writer in the same way I climbed up on this platform: I was coerced.' In his third effort, when he received the Rómulo Gallegos Prize in 1972, he confirms that he has agreed 'to do two of the things . . . that I'd promised myself I would never do: accept a prize and give a speech'.*

Ten years later, Gabriel García Márquez received the Nobel Prize in Literature and found himself in urgent need of writing the most important speech a writer can ever give in his life. The result was a masterpiece: 'The Solitude of Latin America'. From then on, the genre became essential in his career as an admired, award-winning author whose presence and words were requested all around the world.

In this edition I have had the privilege of working with the author, literally side by side, in revising the texts. The changes have been the usual orthographic and typographical ones, and his decision to give titles to some speeches that until now had been known by the occasion on which they were delivered, such as the one for the Rómulo Gallegos Prize, which he calls here 'Because of You'. Rereading these scattered or forgotten texts, in a genre he always considered 'the most terrifying of human commitments', has led García Márquez to be reconciled with them and to remark: 'Reading these speeches, I've rediscovered how I have changed and evolved as a writer.' Not only are the central themes of his literature concentrated in them but also the clues that help us understand his life more deeply.

We are grateful to Gabriel García Márquez and his wife, Mercedes Barcha, for their continuing hospitality and generosity during the working sessions that allowed us to finish this book. And to their sons, Rodrigo and Gonzalo, for their passionate, long-distance interest in discovering a forgotten speech or sharing their opinions regarding titles or book jackets. Finally, my thanks to Professor Anibal González-Pérez, of Yale University, for joining me in the editing of this book and for finding the speech that opens it.

Cristóbal Pera

NOTES ON THE SPEECHES

The Academy of Duty
Zipaquirá, Colombia, November 17, 1944

At the farewell to the class of 1944, a year ahead of García Márquez's, which graduated with the *bachillerato* from the Liceo Nacional de Varones de Zipaquirá (National Secondary School for Boys of Zipaquirá). Thanks to a scholarship, Gabriel García Márquez was able to continue his studies as a boarder at the Liceo Nacional de Varones de Zipaquirá.

How I Began to Write
Caracas, Venezuela, May 3, 1970

At the Athenaeum of Caracas. Published afterwards in *El Espectador* of Bogotá. According to Juan Carlos Zapata in his article '*Gabo nació en Caracas, no en Aracataca*' ('Gabo was Born in Caracas, not Aracataca'), Nicolás Trincado, the journalist, went to the forum as soon as he learned that Gabriel García

Márquez would take part, and there he found him, 'skinny, thickly moustached, with a lit cigarette'.

Because of You
Caracas, Venezuela, August 2, 1972

Upon receiving the Second International Rómulo Gallegos
Novel Prize for *One Hundred Years of Solitude*

In the Paris Theatre. The members of the jury were Mario Vargas Llosa, Antonia Palacios, Emir Rodríguez Monegal, José Luis Cano, and Domingo Miliani. García Márquez gave the prize money ($22,000) to the Movimiento al Socialismo (MAS; Movement towards Socialism). The money was used to found the newspaper *Punto*. In addition to the winner, the press mentioned the following novels as finalists: *A Meditation*, by Juan Benet; *Three Sad Tigers*, by Guillermo Cabrera Infante; and *When I Want to Cry I Don't Cry*, by Miguel Otero Silva.

Another, Different Homeland
Mexico City, October 22, 1982

After receiving the Orden del Águila Azteca
(Order of the Aztec Eagle) Insignia Rank

In the Salón Venustiano Carranza of Los Pinos, before the President of the Republic, José López Portillo y Pacheco, and the Chancellor of Colombia, Ramiro Lloreda. According to protocol, the Chancellor of Mexico, Jorge Castañeda, bestowed the order on García Márquez. This is the highest award the Mexican government can grantto a foreigner.

The Solitude of Latin America

Stockholm, Sweden, December 8, 1982

Ceremony awarding the Nobel Prize
in Literature to Gabriel García Márquez

In the Stockholm Concert Hall. The novelist and six scientists — Kenneth G. Wilson (Physics), Aaron Klug (Chemistry), Sune K. Bergström, Bengt Samuelsson, and John R. Vane (Medicine), and George J. Stigler (Economics) — received the prestigious award from the hands of the Swedish king, Carl XVI Gustaf, and his wife, Silvia. In addition to being the central figure of the ceremony, Gabriel García Márquez broke with a tradition in the history of the Nobel Prizes by appearing in typical Caribbean clothing, known as a *liqui-liqui*, instead of the formal white tie and tails.

A Toast to Poetry

Stockholm, Sweden, December 10, 1982

During the royal banquet offered by the
king and queen of Sweden in honour of those
who had received the Nobel Prizes

The gala supper was held in the Blue Room of the Stockholm City Hall. In his article entitled '*La suerte de no hacer colas*' ('The Luck of Not Standing in Line'), published May 4, 1983, and collected in *Press Notes, Journalistic Work 5, 1961–84*, García Márquez recalls: 'They asked me to sign a printed form ceding to the Nobel Foundation the author's rights to my acceptance speech and my toast to poetry – which in a last-minute rush I had improvised for four hands with the poet Álvaro Mutis – and then I signed copies of my books in Swedish for employees of the foundation . . .'

Words for a New Millennium

Havana, Cuba, November 29, 1985

Second Meeting of Intellectuals for the
Sovereignty of the Peoples of Our America

The main address of the opening session of the meeting, at the headquarters of Casa de las Américas. Present were Frei Betto, Ernesto Cardenal, Juan Bosch, Daniel Viglietti, and Osvaldo Soriano, among three hundred other intellectuals from the continent.

The Cataclysm of Damocles

Ixtapa–Zihuatanejo, Mexico, August 6, 1986

Second Summit Meeting of the Group of Six

The opening speech of the meeting of the Group of Six – Argentina, Mexico, Tanzania, Greece, India, and Sweden – on peace and disarmament in the face of the nuclear threat, with the presence of member-country presidents Raúl Alfonsín of Argentina and Miguel de la Madrid Hurtado of Mexico, and prime ministers Andreas Papandreou of Greece, Ingvar Carlsson of Sweden, Rajiv Gandhi of India, and Julius Nyerere of Tanzania.

An Indestructible Idea

Havana, Cuba, December 4, 1986

At the opening ceremony of the headquarters of the Foundation for a New Latin American Cinema

At the foundation, located on the former country estate of Santa Bárbara, in an old mansion in the Marianao district, the Escuela Internacional de Cine, Televisión, y Video (EICTV; International School of Cinema, Television, and Video) of San Antonio de los Baños, also known as the 'Escuela de Tres Mundos' ('Three Worlds School'). Gabriel García Márquez spoke in his capacity as foundation president.

Preface to a New Millennium

Caracas, Venezuela, March 4, 1990

Opening of the exhibition *Figuration and Fabulation:*
Seventy-five years of Painting in Latin America, 1914–89

The exhibition was shown at the Museum of Fine Arts,
curated by the Venezuelan critic Roberto Guevara and
coordinated by Milagros Maldonado. The speech was used
as the prologue to the exhibition catalogue.

Artists taking part were Antonio Barrera and Álvaro Bar-
rios, Colombia; José Bedia, Cuba; Sirón Franco, Brazil; Julio
Galán, Mexico; Guillermo Kuitca, Argentina; Ana Mendi-
eta, Cuba; Juan Vicente Hernández (*Pájaro*), Venezuela;
Pancho Quilici, Venezuela; Arnaldo Roche, Puerto Rico;
Antônio José de Mello Mourão (*Tunga*), Brazil; and Carlos
Zerpa, Venezuela.

I'm Not Here

Havana, Cuba, December 8, 1992

Inauguration of the screening room of the
Foundation for the New Latin American Cinema

The Glauber Rocha screening room forms part of the cultural centre at the headquarters of the Foundation for the
New Latin American Cinema. In this room, a cultural centre
in itself, not only are films shown but national and international seminars and conferences held, theatrical works

produced, and dance recitals and chamber music concerts presented.

In Honour of Belisario Betancur on the Occasion of His Seventieth Birthday
Santafé de Bogotá, Colombia, February 18, 1993

The celebration took place in José Asunción Silva Poetry House. The convocation to the celebration of the seventieth birthday of the former president of Colombia, born on February 4, was signed, among others, by Gabriel García Márquez, Álvaro Mutis, Alfonso López Michelsen, Germán Arciniegas, Germán Espinosa, Abelardo Forero Benavides, Hernando Valencia Goelkel, Rafael Gutiérrez Girardot, Antonio Caballero, Darío Jaramillo Agudelo, and María Mercedes Carranza, director of the José Asunción Silva Poetry House.

My Friend Mutis
Santafé de Bogotá, Colombia, August 25, 1993

On the occasion of the seventieth birthday of Álvaro Mutis

Read by Gabriel García Márquez to his friend Álvaro Mutis at the gala dinner held on the occasion of his seventieth birthday at Nariño House, Bogotá, seat of the presidency of Colombia, where the government of President César Gaviria awarded Mutis the Cruz de Boyacá (Order of Boyacá). On

November 26, 2007, within the framework of the Twenty-second Guadalajara Book Fair, dedicated to Colombia, tribute was paid to Álvaro Mutis, and former president Belisario Betancur read this text 'with the permission of García Márquez', who was sitting beside him.

The Argentine who Endeared Himself to Everybody
Palace of Fine Arts, Mexico City, February 12, 1994

The speech – first published as an article on February 22, 1984, a few days after the death of Julio Cortázar – was a tribute to the author ten years after that date. The same text would be read at the opening round table of the colloquium 'Julio Cortázar Revisited', February 14, 2004, in Guadalajara, Jalisco, in the tribute by the Julio Cortázar Chair at the University of Guadalajara, presided over by Gabriel García Márquez and Carlos Fuentes, twenty years after the death of the Argentine writer.

Latin America Exists
Contadora, Panama, March 28, 1995

'Laboratory' of the Contadora Group on the topic
'Does Latin America Exist?'

Present were the former president of Uruguay, Luis Alberto Lacalle, as moderator, and, as participants, Federico Mayor

Zaragoza, Gabriel García Márquez (who was the last speaker at the meeting), Miguel de la Madrid Hurtado (former president of Mexico), Sergio Ramírez (former vice-president of Nicaragua), Francisco Weffort (Minister of Culture of Brazil), and Augusto Ramírez Ocampo (former Chancellor of Colombia).

Within the context of the crisis buffeting Central America, the Contadora Group was born on January 9, 1983, to contribute to peace and democracy in the region; its first members were Colombia, Mexico, Panama, and Venezuela. The group took its name from the Panamanian island where the chancellors of these four countries met to found the group.

A Different Nature in a World Different from Ours
Santafé de Bogotá, Colombia, April 12, 1996

Chair of Colombia

The Colombian armed forces officially inaugurated the programme called the Chair of Colombia with the conference 'A Government of Laws and Public Force', under the direction of then Colombian minister of national defence, Juan Carlos Esguerra Portocarrero.

Before an audience composed of military personnel, the speakers included Gabriel García Márquez, Rodrigo Pardo García, the public prosecutor Alfonso Valdivieso Sarmiento, the historian Germán Arciniegas, the former ministers Juan Manuel Santos and Rudolf Hommes Rodríguez, the former

assembly member Orlando Fals Borda, and the writer
Gustavo Álvarez Gardeazábal.

Journalism: The Best Job in the World
Los Angeles, United States, October 7, 1996

Fifty-second Assembly of the Sociedad Interamericana de Prensa
(SIP; Inter-American Press Society),
with headquarters in Miami, Florida

Opening speech given by Gabriel García Márquez in his
capacity as president of the Foundation for a New Ibero-
American Journalism.

A Bottle in the Ocean for the God of Words
Zacatecas, Mexico, April 7, 1997

First International Congress on the Spanish Language

The winner of the Nobel Prize in Literature, to whom the
congress was paying tribute, spoke at the opening of the congress and provoked a considerable polemic when he
challenged adherence to orthography.

Dreams for the Twenty-first Century
Paris, France, March 8, 1999

Seminar: 'Latin America and the
Caribbean Facing the New Millennium'

The Inter-American Bank for Development and UNESCO organized in Paris, on March 8 and 9, the seminar 'Latin America and the Caribbean Facing the New Millennium'. Gabriel García Márquez, a special guest of the meeting, gave this brief inaugural address.

The Beloved Though Distant Homeland
Medellín, Colombia, May 18, 2003

International symposium: 'Towards a New
Social Contract in Science and Technology
for Equitable Development'

At the ceremony commemorating the two hundredth anniversary of the University of Antioquia, this text was recorded with the voice of Gabriel García Márquez and a copy of it was sent to Medellín, where it was broadcast at 6 p.m. on the opening day of the symposium, in the Teatro Camilo Torres.

A Soul Open to be Filled with Messages in Spanish

Cartagena de Indias, Colombia, March 26, 2007

Before the Academies of the
Language and the king and queen of Spain

In the Convention Centre of Cartagena, during the opening of the Fourth International Congress of the Language, in a tribute to Gabriel García Márquez. The author had turned eighty on March 6, the fortieth anniversary of the publication of *One Hundred Years of Solitude* was being celebrated with a commemorative edition, and it was the twenty-fifth anniversary of his Nobel Prize.